Englisch

7./8. Klasse

Verena Rotter

If-Sätze und Futurformen

Mit heraustrennbarem Lösungsteil

Mentor Übungsbuch 855

Mentor Verlag München

Die Autorin: Verena Rotter, Lehrerin für Englisch, Kunsterziehung, Werken und Technisches Zeichnen

Redaktion: Ulrike Timmer

Illustrationen: Henning Schöttke, Kiel

In neuer Rechtschreibung

Umwelthinweis: Gedruckt auf chlorfrei gebleichtem Papier

Layout: Peter Glaubitz, auf der Basis des Layouts von Barbara Slowik, München
Umschlag: Iris Steiner, München
Satz: OK Satz GmbH, Unterschleißheim
Druck: Landesverlag Druckservice, Linz

1. 2. 3. 05 04 03

Inhaltsverzeichnis

Vorwort   5

A   Futurformen   6
  1. Will-Future für Vermutungen und Vorhersagen   6
  2. Will-Future für spontane Entschlüsse und Angebote   8
  3. Going to-Future 10
  4. Will-Future und going to-Future im Vergleich 12
  5. Will-Future und going to-Future: Mixed Exercises 14
  6. Simple Present mit zukünftiger Bedeutung 16
  7. Present Progressive mit zukünftiger Bedeutung 18
  8. Gegenwartsformen mit zukünftiger Bedeutung im Vergleich 20
  9. Future Progressive 22
 10. Future Perfect 24
 11. Futurformen im Überblick 26
 12. Abschlusstest Futurformen 28

B   If-Sätze 30
  1. Grundlagen 30
  2. Typ I mit will-Future 32
  3. Typ I mit Imperativ oder modalem Hilfsverb 34
  4. Typ I: Mixed Exercises 36
  5. Typ II mit unwahrscheinlicher Bedingung 38
  6. Typ II mit unmöglicher Bedingung 40
  7. Typ I und Typ II im Vergleich 42
  8. Typ III 44
  9. Unmögliche Bedingungen im Vergleich (Typ II und Typ III) 46
 10. Typ I, Typ II und Typ III im Vergleich 48
 11. Abschlusstest if-Sätze 50
 12. Sonderformen 52

Lösungsteil 55

Unser Tipp für alle, die noch mehr wissen wollen:

Mentor Lernhilfen

Die sind Spezialisten im Erklären und machen fit fürs ganze Schuljahr!

Für Englisch in der 7./8. Klasse gibt's die Bände:

Keep it up! 1 (7./8. Klasse)
Ein Übungsprogramm für Grammatik und Wortschatz 1
ISBN 3-580-63545-X

Keep it up! 2 (7./8. Klasse)
Ein Übungsprogramm für Grammatik und Wortschatz 2
ISBN 3-580-63546-8

Vorwort

Hallo, liebe Schülerin, lieber Schüler,

du möchtest dein Englisch ein bisschen trainieren, aber möglichst gezielt und mit Erfolg? Dann bist du hier richtig – egal, ob du dich nun generell verbessern oder eines der Themen dieses Buches speziell üben willst.

Und so funktioniert's:

Treffsicher — Dieses Buch ist in **24 kleine Lernportionen** gegliedert.
→ So findest du dich besonders schnell zurecht.

Übersichtlich — Jede Lernportion umfasst genau eine **Doppelseite**.
→ So hast du immer alles auf einen Blick.

Einleuchtend — Jede Doppelseite beginnt mit einer kurzen, klaren **Regel**.
→ So weißt du immer sofort, worauf es ankommt.

Clever — Dann geht's ans **Üben** – ganz locker, Schritt für Schritt.
→ So bereitest du dich optimal vor.

Praktisch — Der **Lösungsteil** zum Heraustrennen passt seitengetreu dazu.
→ So kontrollierst du blitzschnell – ohne Suchen und Blättern.

Am besten gleich loslegen!

Aber Pausen nicht vergessen!

Viel Spaß und ganz viel Erfolg

wünscht dir

dein Mentor Verlag

Noch ein Tipp — Du hast noch mehr Nachholbedarf, aber keine Lust auf Nachhilfe? Dann versuch's doch mit den **Mentor Lernhilfen**: Schau mal auf die Seite gegenüber!

Futurformen

Im Englischen gibt es eine Reihe verschiedener Möglichkeiten, zukünftige Geschehen auszudrücken. Welche Zukunftsform man verwendet, hängt davon ab, ob es sich z. B. um ein schon länger geplantes Vorhaben oder um einen spontanen Entschluss, einen offiziellen Zeitplan oder eine persönliche Verabredung handelt.

1. Will-future für Vermutungen und Vorhersagen

Verwendung
a) für Vorhersagen → *The weather will be nice tomorrow.*
b) für Vermutungen → *I think Dad will be late today.*

Bildung:
bejahter Satz
will + Grundform → *Dinner will be ready in twenty*
(Kurzform: *'ll*)   *minutes.*
verneinter Satz
will + *not* + Grundform → *We won't have soup today.*
(Kurzform: *won't*)
Fragesatz
(Fragewort +) *will* + → *Will Ben pass his driving test?*
Subjekt + Grundform

Merke

Signalwörter
a) *tomorrow, in (3 weeks), next (summer), in (2007)*
b) *I think, I'm sure, probably, perhaps*

Übung 1

Familie Parker aus Reading lauscht dem Wetterbericht. Wie wird das Wetter morgen in Großbritannien? Setze die richtige Verbform ein.

Tomorrow it ....be........ (be) warm and sunny in South England. There

.......be........ (be) light winds from the South-West only.

The Midlands ....be........ (be) cloudy, but it .....stays..... (stay) dry.

It _rains_ (rain) heavily in Scotland tomorrow.

In the Highlands there _be_ (be) strong winds from the North-West and the temperature there _not go_ (not go) above 8°C.

In Wales it _be_ (be) cloudy, but it _not rain_ (not rain) all day.

You _even have_ (even, have) some sunny spells *(dt. sonnige Abschnitte)* in the early evening.

In Northern Ireland it _be_ (be) cloudy with lots of rain.

Temperatures _not climb_ (not climb) above 10°C.

Übung 2

Die 13-jährige Sarah Parker schreibt einen Aufsatz zum Thema „When I'm thirty". Bilde aus ihrer „Stoffsammlung" Sätze.

earn lots of money → I will _earn lots of money_.

have husband and children → _I will have a husband and children._

have to cook dinner for my family → _I have to cook dinner for my family_

not have to be at home at 8 p.m. → _I not have to be home at 8 p.m._

not go to bed at 10 p.m. → _I will not go to bed at 10 p.m._

my parents be over 60 → _My Parents will be over 60_.

Übung 3

Sarahs deutsche Brieffreundin Laura will von einer berühmten englischen Wahrsagerin Auskünfte über ihre Zukunft … Übersetze ihre Fragen ins Englische.

1. Werde ich mich bald verlieben *(engl. fall in love)*?

   Will I fall in love soon

2. Werde ich gute Noten bekommen?

   Will i get good Notes

3. Wird Petra wirklich aus München wegziehen?

   Will Petra really move away from Munich

4. Werde ich ein Snowboard zu meinem Geburtstag bekommen?

   Will i get a Snowboard for my Birthday

2. Will-Future für spontane Entschlüsse und Angebote

Verwendung

c) für spontane Entschlüsse, die erst im Moment des Sprechens gefasst werden

    (A: Oh, I forgot the milk.)
    → *B: No problem, I'll go and buy some.*

d) für Angebote und Vorschläge: *shall* (dt. sollen) → wird nur mit *I* und *we* verwendet!

    → *Shall I open the window?*
    Shall we go swimming today?

e) nach bestimmten Verben, die in die Zukunft weisen, z. B. *expect, hope, promise, wonder, suppose* (dt. annehmen)

    → *I promise I'll be back at 9 p.m.*

Beachte:
Das englische will-Future wird im Deutschen oft mit dem Präsens wiedergegeben:
I'll go and buy some bread.   → Ich geh' und kaufe etwas Brot.

Nicht verwechseln:

I will go now.	↔	*I want* to go now.
Ich werde jetzt gehen. /	↔	Ich will jetzt gehen.
Ich gehe jetzt.		

Übung 1

Am *Mother's Day* wollen Sarah, Steve und Ben Parker ihrer Mutter jeden Wunsch erfüllen. Schwester Julie ist krank und könnte die Überraschung verderben.
Finde das passende Verb und setze es in die richtige Form.
buy – do – sit – stay – go

1. Mrs Parker: "Look at all these dirty dishes ..."

   Sarah: "I ____do____ the washing-up for you, Mum."

2. Mrs Parker: "We haven't got any biscuits."

   Ben: "No problem, Mum, I ____go____ and buy some."

3. Mrs Parker: "Yesterday I dropped my favourite bottle of perfume on the floor and broke it."
   Ben & Steve: "We ____buy____ a new bottle for you."

4. Mrs Parker: "I'd like to go out with Fred tonight, but Julie is ill ..."

   Sarah & Steve: "We ____stay____ at home and we ____sit____ at her bedside all night, Mum."

Übung 2

Übersetze ins Deutsche, was Mrs Parker noch zu Steve und Sarah sagt, als sie und ihr Mann abends das Haus verlassen.

1. I promise we'll return at 11 p.m.

   Ich verspreche das ich am 11 Uhr zurück komme

2. I hope there won't be a traffic jam (dt. Stau).

   I hoffe das dort keint Stau seien wird.

3. I suppose Julie's temperature won't rise any (hier: dt. noch) further (dt. weiter).

   I denke Julie Temperatur wird nicht noch weiter stegen

4. I expect Julie will fall asleep soon.

   Außerdem denke ich Julie wird bald einschlafen

Übung 3

Als Mr und Mrs Parker weggegangen sind, machen Sarah und Steve der 8-jährigen Julie ein paar Vorschläge, was sie machen könnten. Was haben sie auf Englisch gesagt?

1. Julie: „Mir ist so langweilig. Was sollen wir heute Abend machen?"

   "I'm so bored. *What shall we do Evening today ?* "

2. Sarah: „Soll ich dir eine Tasse Tee holen?"

   Sarah: „Shod i get you a coup of tee ?"

3. Steve: „Soll ich den Fernseher anmachen?"

   Steve: „Shod i turn the TV an ?"

4. Sarah & Steve: „Sollen wir dir eine Geschichte vorlesen?"

   Sarah & Steve: „shawd we read a story to you?"

5. Steve: „Soll ich dein Malbuch (engl. colouring book) bringen?"

   Steve: „Showd i bring you your colouringbook ?"

Übung 4

Sarah will in einem Brief „testen", ob Laura schon die verschiedenen Aspekte des will-Future kennt. Kannst du ihr bei der Zuordnung helfen?

1. Shall we go to the cinema tonight?
2. I wonder what the film will be like.
3. There will be seven billion (dt. Milliarden) people on our planet soon.
4. A: I like this sweater. – B: I'll buy it for you.
5. I think Sarah will get a good mark in her German test.

a) Vorhersage
b) Vermutung
c) spontanes Angebot
d) Vorschlag
e) will-Future nach bestimmten Verben

3. Going to-Future

Verwendung
- für feste, bereits länger bestehende Pläne, Absichten und Vorsätze

  → We're going to visit Grandma on Sunday.

- für absehbare Ereignisse (Anzeichen sind vorhanden)

  → (Look at these black clouds.) It is going to rain soon.

Bildung:
bejahter Satz
am / are / is + going to + Grundform

→ Steve is going to learn canoeing in the summer holidays.

verneinter Satz
am / are / is + not + going to + Grundform

→ I'm not going to do the washing-up alone again.

Fragesatz
(Fragewort +) am / are / is + Subjekt + going to + Grundform

→ Is Sarah going to stay overnight at Vicky's house?

Beachte:
Das going to-Future verwendet man <u>nicht</u> bei *come* und *go*.
Hier bevorzugt man das Present Progressive (vgl. Kap. 7).
My cousin is coming this afternoon. We are going swimming.

Übung 1

Nach Julie ist Mrs Parker krank geworden. Die Kinder haben nun viel zu erledigen. – Ergänze den Dialog.

Mrs Parker: Steve, have you done the shopping yet?

Steve: Not yet, Mum. I _____do_____ (do) it later.

Mrs Parker: Sarah, have you cleaned the rooms yet?

Sarah: I've cleaned Ben and Steve's room as well as mine. But Julie's room looks such a mess. I _____not clean_____ (not clean) it.

Mrs Parker: I've just talked to her. She _____cleans_____ (clean) the room herself.

Sarah: Has she got time to do it? It's her turn to scrub *(dt. schrubben)* the kitchen floor, isn't it?

Mrs Parker: You are right, Sarah. It *is* her turn, but she _____not srubs_____ (not scrub) the floor. She said she's still too ill ...

Übung 2

Mrs Parker hat einen schlimmen Albtraum. Gleich wird etwas passieren! Vervollständige die Sätze mit dem passenden Verb in der richtigen Form.

flood *(dt. überschwemmen)*   **boil over** *(dt. überkochen)*   **have**   **fall off**

1. Julie has put milk onto the stove. She forgets to turn the hot-plate *(dt. Herdplatte)* off.

   The milk _____ boils over

2. Steve and Eric are climbing up an old ladder to pick apples. One rung *(dt. Sprosse)* of

   the ladder is loose. They _____ fall off _____ the ladder.

3. Sarah is running a bath (run a bath, *dt. sich ein Bad einlaufen lassen*).
   She leaves the bathroom and talks to her friend Vicky on the phone for an hour.

   The water _____ floods _____ the whole house.

4. Ben is driving a car without a driver's licence *(dt. Führerschein)*. He hasn't slept for

   24 hours. He _____ have _____ an accident.

Übung 3

Sarah und ihr Zwillingsbruder Steve werden bald 14. Laura möchte wissen, wie sie feiern werden. Kannst du ihr helfen den Brief auf Englisch zu verfassen?

Liebe Sarah,
in deinem letzten Brief hast du geschrieben, dass du zusammen mit Steve eine große Party geben wirst …

Wo werdet ihr feiern *(engl. celebrate)*?
Wen wirst du einladen *(engl. invite)*?

Welche Musik werdet ihr spielen?

Wird deine Mutter wieder ihre köstlichen Salate machen?

Was wirst du Steve zum Geburtstag schenken (= geben)? Ich wünschte, ich könnte mit euch feiern.

Deine Laura

Dear Sarah,
You wrote in your last letter that you

_____ a big party together with Steve …

Where will you celebrate?
Wroow you gona invite?

What kind of music will you play ?
Will your Mother make her delicious salads again?
What will you give Steve for his birthday? I wish I could celebrate with you.

Yours, Laura

4. Will-Future und going to-Future im Vergleich

Verwendung:

will-Future	going to-Future
• für spontane Entschlüsse (die Entscheidung fällt im Moment des Sprechens) A: *This is a beautiful sweater.* B: *I'll buy it for you.*	• für länger gehegte Pläne (die Entscheidung fiel schon vor dem Moment des Sprechens) *I'm going to buy a pair of shoes this afternoon.*
• für zukünftige Ereignisse, die man nicht beeinflussen kann *It will rain tomorrow.* *The twins will be 14 next week.*	• für zukünftige Ereignisse, die man selbst bestimmen kann *Sarah is going to visit her grandma tomorrow.*
• für reine Vermutungen *I think Steve will like our present.* • für Angebote und Vorschläge • nach bestimmten Verben	• für absehbare Ereignisse (Anzeichen sind vorhanden) *Tom has been too lazy.* *He is going to fail his exams.*

Merke

Signalwörter:

will-Future	going to-Future
• *probably, perhaps, I think, I'm sure* • Textzusammenhänge, die deutlich machen, dass die Entscheidung erst im Moment des Sprechens gefällt wird	• Textzusammenhänge, die darauf hinweisen, dass die Entscheidung schon vorher getroffen wurde

Übung 1 **Welche Pläne hast du für heute Abend, nächstes Wochenende und die Ferien? Wie sieht's mit deinen Eltern, Freunden und Geschwistern aus? Bilde Sätze.**

I my parents my brother / my sister my friend	watch TV / read ? play ? visit ? ? *learn*	tonight next weekend in the holidays *know*

1. I'm learning English in the holidays.
2. My parents play Music tonight

3. My Brother visits Amerika in the holidays

4. My Sisters play know

5. My friend visit's me tonight

6.

7.

Übung 2

Sarah und Steve brauchen noch ein paar *„helping hands"* für ihre Party. Ein paar Freunde bieten spontan ihre Hilfe an. Welche Futurform passt hier?

1. Sarah: "We haven't got enough biscuits."

   Vicky: "I ____ bake ____ (bake) some."

2. Steve: "We've only got fifteen CDs."

   Joe: "I ____ bring ____ (bring) my CD collection."

3. Sarah: "Oh no! I've dropped the chocolate cake!"

   Karen & Amy: "Never mind. We ____ make ____ (make) a new one."

4. Steve: "Look! We've only got twenty glasses. We need another ten or twelve."

   Susan: "No problem. I ____ go ____ (go) and get you twenty if you like."

Übung 3

Vor der Party unterhalten sich Freunde von Steve und Sarah. Bilde Sätze in der wörtlichen Rede. Verwende die richtigen Futurformen.

1. Karen fragt Vicky, ob sie denkt, dass Sarah ihr Geschenk gefallen wird.

   Karen: "Vicky, ____ do you think, that Sarah will like ____ our present?"

2. Vicky ist sich sicher, dass sie es lieben wird.

   Vicky: "I'm ____ sure, she will love ____ it."

3. Eric fragt Justin, was er Steve schenken (= geben) wird.

   Eric: "What ____ will you give ____ Steve?"

4. Justin antwortet, dass er ihm ein Poster von Andre Agassi schenken wird.

   Justin: "I ____ will give him ____ a poster of Andre Agassi."

5. Justin fügt hinzu, dass er annimmt, dass Steve es sich an die Wand hängen wird.

   Justin: "I ____ onto the wall."

5. Will-Future und going to-Future: Mixed Exercises

Übung 1   Mr und Mrs Parker sind auch zur Party gekommen und machen eine Reihe von Vorschlägen und Angeboten.
Bilde Sätze.

1. Vicky: "It's really hot in here."

   Mrs Parker: "_Shod i open the window_ (I, open, window)?"

2. Sarah: "I've been dancing for two hours. I'm completely exhausted."

   Mr Parker: "_Shoud i get you a chair_ (I, get, you, chair)?"

3. Steve: "I think we're running out of lemonade."

   Mr & Mrs Parker: "_Wi_ (we, go) and get some more?"

4. Eric: "I hate this techno music."

   Mr Parker: "_Showd i live play_ (I, play) one of my Beatles cassettes?"

5. Amy: "I have to be home at 10 p.m. But my parents can't collect me because they haven't got a car this week."

   Mrs Parker: "_Sheee i drive youhome_ (I, drive, you, home)?"

6. Sarah: "Karen would like to stay overnight."

   Mrs Parker: "_Showd i make aguest bed_ (I, make, guest bed) for her?"

Übung 2   Sarah und Steve haben von ihrer Großmutter zum Geburtstag Geld bekommen. Als sie zwei Wochen später wieder kommt, möchte sie wissen, was Sarah und Steve damit vorhaben.
Verwende die richtigen Futurformen.

Grandma: Well, Steve and Sarah, what _will you do_ (you, do) with the money I gave you?

Sarah: I've already decided that I _save_ (save) half of it.

Grandma: And what about the other half?

Sarah: I haven't had the time to spend it yet, but I _definitely buy_ (definitely, buy) the brand new *Spice Girls* CD.

Grandma: And what _you do_ (you, do) with the rest?

Sarah: I _give_ (give) Mum and Dad tickets for the theatre because they helped us so much with our party.

Grandma: That's very nice of you, Sarah. And what _will you do_ (you, do) with the money, Steve?

Steve: Well, unlike Sarah, I _____certainly not save_____ (certainly, not, save) any of it.

Grandma: What _____you buy_____ (you, buy) then?

Steve: I haven't thought about it so far. Perhaps I _____buy_____ (buy) a pair of new tennis shoes. I hope I _____find_____ (find) nice ones. And tomorrow I _____do_____ (do) a cycling tour with James and Eric. I'm sure I _____need_____ (need) some money.

Grandma: Have you listened to the weather forecast?

Steve: Yes, I have. It _____be_____ (be) cloudy but it _____ee not_____ _____rain_____ (not, rain).

Übung 3

Hier kommt der Expertentest:
Kannst du jeweils begründen, warum das Futur mit *will / shall* bzw. *going to* gebildet werden muss?

1. It will be rather cold tomorrow.   → Vorhersage → *will*

2. Shall we go swimming?   → Frage → Shall

3. I'm going to watch a video tonight.   → Entscheidung → going to

4. I promise I'll be back in 5 minutes.   → Vermutung → will

5. Look at the sky. It's going to rain.   → Vorhersage → going to

6. I think Ben will pass the test easily.   → Vermutung → will

7. (A: I'm too tired to do the shopping.)

   B: No problem. I'll do it for you.   → Entschluss → will

6. Simple Present mit zukünftiger Bedeutung

Mit dem Simple Present kann man nicht nur regelmäßige Handlungen in der Gegenwart zum Ausdruck bringen, man verwendet es auch, um über bereits festgelegte zukünftige Ereignisse zu sprechen.

Verwendung

- für zukünftige Geschehen, die durch Fahr- und sonstige Zeitpläne, Kalender, Programme etc. festgelegt sind
  → *Mrs Parker's train leaves at 4.30 p.m.*
- → typische Verben hierfür sind: *arrive, begin, close, end, finish, leave, open, start, stop*
  → *He arrives in Birmingham at 6.30 p.m.*
- in Nebensätzen der Bedingung (Typ I) und der Zeit, die sich auf die Zukunft beziehen (im Hauptsatz → *will-future*)
  → *If the weather is nice tomorrow, Steve and his friends will enjoy their cycling tour.*
- → Konjunktionen: *if, when, while, before, as soon as, not ... until*
  → *Steve will phone his parents as soon as they get to the youth hostel.*

Bildung
Verb in der Grundform
bei der 3. Pers. Sing.: + *-(e)s*
  → *The museums close at 4 p.m.*
  → *The film finishes at 9.30 p.m.*

Beachte:
Umschreibung mit *do / does* in Frage und Verneinung
  → *When does the museum open?*

Merke

Signalwörter
Datums- und Zeitangaben, z. B. *on (May 17th)*, *at (4 o'clock)*

Übung 1

**Steve und seine Freunde wollen mit dem Bus in die Stadt.
Ergänze ihre Unterhaltung mit Mr Hill, dem Herbergsvater.**

Steve: Excuse me, Mr Hill, when ...... *does* ...... the next bus to the city centre ...... *leave* ...... (leave)?

Mr Hill: It ...... *leaves* ...... (leave) in about ten minutes. What are you going to visit?

Eric: Well, first of all we'd like to go on a sight-seeing tour. Do you know where the tours start?

Mr Hill: They _start_ (start) in front of the town hall on the hour.

Steve: And I'd like to go to the *British Handcraft Museum*.

Mr Hill: You'll have to hurry then, boys. The museum _closes_ (close) at 4 o'clock.

Eric: And when _does it open_ (it, open) tomorrow morning? Just in case we don't manage to get there in time …

Mr Hill: I think it _opens_ (open) at 9 a.m. I can check that for you.
Why don't you go to the inline-disco tonight?

James: Inline-disco? Great! Where _does it take place_ (it, take place, *dt. stattfinden)* and when _does it begin_ (it, begin)?

Mr Hill: It's in the sports centre in Beechwood Road. And it _starts_ (start) at 8 p.m. and _finishes_ (finish) at 11 p.m. But don't forget that the youth hostel _closes_ (close) at 10.30 p.m.

Übung 2   Bilde Sätze mit den angegebenen Konjunktionen. Achte auf die richtige Zeitform in Haupt- und Nebensatz.

1. Steve / go to bed / as soon as / he / return / from the cycling tour
   Steve goes to bed as soon as he returns from cycling tour

2. Sarah / take a shower / before / she / go to the cinema
   Sarah takes a shower before she goes to the cinema

3. Mr Parker / phone / his wife / when / he / arrive in Birmingham
   Mr Parkers phones his wife when he arrives in Birmingham

4. The children / not / start / breakfast / until / their parents / sit down at the table
   The children dont start breakfast until their parents sit down at the table

A 7. Present Progressive mit zukünftiger Bedeutung

Das Present Progressive kann nicht nur gerade ablaufende Handlungen beschreiben, es kann auch Zukünftiges ausdrücken.

Verwendung
- für feste Verabredungen und Pläne in der (nahen) Zukunft
  → *Steve is playing tennis tomorrow morning.*

Bildung:
bejahter Satz
am / are / is + Grundform + *-ing*
  → *Ben is watching TV tonight.*
verneinter Satz
am / are / is + *not* + Grundform + *-ing*
  → *Mr and Mrs Parker aren't watching the film tonight.*
Fragesatz
(Fragewort +) *am / are / is* + Subjekt + *Grundform* + *-ing*
  → *What time is Sarah meeting Vicky tomorrow?*

Merke

Signalwörter
Zeitangaben oder Zeitadverbien der Zukunft, z. B. *tomorrow, next (week), at (8 o'clock / 9.30 p.m.), on (Wednesday)* …

Übung 1

Was haben die Parkers in der kommenden Woche vor? Bilde Sätze im Present Progressive. Verwende, falls nicht angegeben, die Verben *go (to), take (to), have* oder *play*.

	Mr Parker	Mrs Parker	Ben	Sarah	Steve	Julie
Mon						ballet class
Tue					tennis	
Wed	dentist			visit Karen		
Thu			cinema			
Fri	car / garage		basketball			art class
Sat		meet Liz		shopping	tennis	
Sun						walk dog

1. Mr Parker _is going to the dentist_ on Wednesday.

   He _is taking the car to the garage_ on Friday.

2. Mrs Parker _is meeting_ her friend Liz on Saturday.

3. Ben _is going to the cinema_ on Thursday evening.

   On Friday he _is playing basketball_

4. Sarah *in visiting Karen* on Wednesday afternoon.

   She *is going shopping* on Saturday.

5. Steve *is playing tennis* on Tuesday and Saturday.

6. Julie *is having* a ballet class on Monday and an art class on Thursday.

   On Sunday she *is walking* Mrs Pearson's dog.

Übung 2

Samstag Vormittag bei den Parkers …
Vervollständige den Dialog mit den richtigen Verbformen.

Julie: Mum, Jackie has just called. She *is going swimming*
(go swimming) in the afternoon. Can you drive me to the pool?

Mrs Parker: I'm sorry, but I can't. I *am meeting* (meet) Liz at 3 p.m.

Julie: What about Dad? He surely *is not joining* (not, join) you and
Liz, is he?

Mrs Parker: Of course not. But he is busy, too. He *is putting up* (put up)
new shelves (dt. Regale) in his study (dt. Arbeitszimmer).

Julie: That's too bad. But Ben could take me on his motorbike, couldn't he?

Mrs Parker: You needn't ask him, Julie. He's just told me that he and Emma
are watching (watch) videos in the afternoon.
Why *aren't you going* (you, not, go) by bike?

Julie: It's got a puncture (dt. Platten), Mum.

Übung 3

Was hast du für die nächste Zeit schon vor bzw. ausgemacht?
Bilde Sätze im Present Progressive.

1. I *am going plaiden* this afternoon.

2. I *want to read* tonight.

3. My best friend and I *are going to visit* at the weekend.

4. I *am going to learn* next week.

8. Gegenwartsformen mit zukünftiger Bedeutung im Vergleich

Verwendung:

Present Progressive
- für Pläne und zukünftige Verabredungen, die man selbst festgesetzt hat

  Mr and Mrs Parker are going to the theatre tonight.

Simple Present
- für Pläne und zukünftige Ereignisse, die „offiziell" festgelegt sind, wie z. B. Fahrpläne und Programme
  The performance starts at 8 p.m.

Nicht vergessen:
Verlaufsformen können nur von Tätigkeitsverben gebildet werden!

Beachte:
Für die Verwendung der Gegenwartsformen mit zukünftiger Bedeutung gibt es keine eindeutigen Signalwörter.
Achte daher auf den Text- bzw. Satzzusammenhang, um herauszufinden, ob es sich um „offizielle" oder um eigene Pläne handelt!

Übung 1

Sam, ein Junge aus Sarahs Klasse, möchte sich mit Sarah verabreden. – Welche Gegenwartsform mit zukünftiger Bedeutung passt hier? Setze die richtige Verbform ein.

Sam: Hi, Sarah. Would you like to go to the cinema with me tonight?

Sarah: I'd love to, but I can't. I __am playing__ (play) tennis with Steve at 7 p.m.

Sam: That's a pity. How about tomorrow?

Sarah: I'm sorry, but Julie and I __are visiting__ (visit) our grandparents tomorrow evening.

Sam: What about Thursday evening then?

Sarah: I think that's not possible either. On Thursday I'm __helping__ (help) my parents in the garden. You know, there's so much to do in spring time.

        But are *you* free on Friday? Vicky and I __are going__ (go) to the cinema Friday night. You can join us if you like.

Sam: Of course I do …

Übung 2

Es ist Freitag Abend. Sarah, Vicky und Sam haben sich bei den Parkers getroffen und diskutieren noch. – Verwende die passende Gegenwartsform mit zukünftiger Bedeutung.

Sarah: Well, which film would *you* like to watch, Vicky?

Vicky: I'd like to watch *American Beauty*.

Sam: When _is it starting_ (it, start)?

Vicky: It _starts_ (start) at 8 o'clock in the *City House* and at 10 o'clock in the *Odeon*.

Sam: And what time _is it finishing_ (the film, finish)?

Vicky: Well, it _lasts_ (last, *dt. dauern*) 90 minutes, so it _finishs_ (finish) at about 9.30 in the *City House* and at 11.30 in the *Odeon*.

Sarah: The last bus _leaves_ (leave) at 11.15, which means that we can't watch it in the *Odeon*. And we really have to hurry if we want to make it in time for the 8 o'clock performance. It's already 7.25.

Sam: When _is the next bus leaving_ (next bus, leave)?

Sarah: It _leaves_ (leave) at 7.30 and it _arrives_ (arrive) at the cinema at 7.50. Well, hurry up, folks …

Übung 3

**Sarah und Steve gehen nächste Woche auf Klassenfahrt. Laura telefoniert mit Sarah und möchte noch einiges wissen.
Bilde Sätze in der wörtlichen Rede.
Verwende Gegenwartsformen mit zukünftiger Bedeutung.**

Laura möchte wissen …

1. wohin sie fahren

"Where ....?"

2. wie lange sie bleiben

3. ob sie mit dem Reisebus *(engl. coach)* oder dem Zug fahren

4. wann ihr Zug abfährt

5. wann er in Bath ankommt

6. wo sie übernachten (= bleiben)

A 9. Future Progressive

Im Englischen gibt es nicht nur in der Gegenwart und Vergangenheit eine Verlaufsform, sondern auch in der Zukunft.

Verwendung

- für Handlungen, die zu einem bestimmten Zeitpunkt in der Zukunft gerade ablaufen werden
  → *Mr Parker will be having a meeting tomorrow at 10 o'clock.*

- für Zukunftspläne und Beschreibungen von zukünftigen Geschehen
  → *This time next week Sarah will be sitting on the train to Bath.*

- für höfliche Fragen, die sich auf die Zukunft beziehen
  → *Will you be using your computer tomorrow?*

Bildung:

bejahter Satz
will + *be* + Grundform + *-ing*
→ *Sarah and Steve will be spending a week in Bath.*

verneinter Satz
won't + *be* + Grundform + *-ing*
→ *Ben won't be watching TV at 7 o'clock.*

Fragesatz
(Fragewort +) *will* + Subjekt + *be* + Grundform + *-ing*
→ *What will you be doing this weekend?*

Merke

Signalwörter

tonight, tomorrow, next (week), this time next (week) sowie Datums- und Zeitangaben, z. B. *at (11 a.m.), on (November 15th)*

Übung 1

Hier siehst du einen Auszug aus Mr Parkers Terminkalender. Sind die folgenden Aussagen wahr oder falsch? Kreuze an.

9.30–1.00	Meet new team assistant
11.00–1.00	Discuss new project
1.00–2.00	Lunch with Mr Donovan
3.15–4.00	See Mr Jackson
4.00–5.00	Have sales talk *(dt. Verkaufsgespräch)*

	true	false
1. Mr Parker will be having lunch at 2.30 p.m.	○	○
2. Mr Parker will be discussing the new project at 11.30 a.m.	○	○
3. Mr Parker will be meeting the new team assistant at 9 a.m.	○	○
4. Mr Parker will be seeing Mr Jackson before lunch.	○	○
5. Mr Parker will be having a sales talk in the afternoon.	○	○

Übung 2

**Sarah träumt schon von der Klassenfahrt nach Bath.
Bilde Sätze im Future Progressive.**

Next week ...

1. ... I _____ (sleep) in a youth hostel.

2. ... Mum _____ (not prepare) breakfast for me.

3. ... Vicky, Karen and I _____ (have) breakfast together.

4. ... we _____ (visit) the famous Roman baths.

5. ... I _____ (send) a postcard to Laura from Bath.

6. ... Sam and Daniel _____ (live on) cheeseburgers.

7. ... Steve _____ (not play) tennis.

8. ... I _____ (talk to) Vicky for hours.

9. ... I _____ (not sleep) at 10.30 p.m.

10. ... Steve and I _____ (miss) our parents.

Übung 3

**Wie du sicher weißt, sind die Briten immer sehr auf Höflichkeit
bedacht. Kannst du die folgenden Fragen im Future Progressive
bilden?**

1. Was machst du heute Abend?

....

2. Wirst du dir morgen das Tennisspiel anschauen?

....

3. Verwendest du nächste Woche dein Lexikon *(engl. dictionary)*?

....

4. Wann wirst du heute Nachmittag das Haus verlassen?

....

5. Wirst du vor 11 Uhr zurückkommen?

....

6. Wann werdet ihr heute zu Abend essen?

....

Verwendung
- für Ereignisse, die zu einem bestimmten Zeitpunkt in der Zukunft abgeschlossen sein werden
  → *Julie will have finished her homework in ten minutes.*

Bildung:
bejahter Satz
will + have + 3. Form d. Verbs
  → *Next month Mr Parker will have worked in this firm for ten years.*

verneinter Satz
won't + have + 3. Form
  → *Laura won't have received Sarah's postcard by the time Sarah gets home.*

Fragesatz
(Fragewort +) *will + Subjekt + have + 3. Form*
  → *When will you have finished your book?*

Merke

Signalwörter
by (dt. bis) *tomorrow / (7) o'clock / next (Friday) …*
not … until (dt. nicht vor) *next (Sunday) / (10) o'clock …*
in (twenty) minutes / hours …, next (week / month) …, when?

Übung 1

Bald sind es zehn Jahre, dass Mr Parker als Programmierer bei *Top-Soft* arbeitet. Was wird er bis zu seinem Jubiläum alles geleistet haben? Bilde Sätze im Future Perfect.

1. Next month Mr Parker .... (work) about two thousand days in this company.

2. He .... (spend) about three thousand hours on trains, buses and planes.

3. He .... (talk) to more than a thousand different customers.

4. He .... (develop) more than eighty computer programmes.

5. He .... (give) about 250 lectures (give a lecture, dt. einen Vortrag halten).

6. He .... (travel) to forty European cities.

Übung 2

Morgen steht bei den Parkers wieder der Frühjahrsputz an.
Wann wird was von wem (noch nicht) erledigt sein?
Bilde Frage- und Antwortsätze im Future Perfect.

	Mr & Mrs Parker	Ben & Steve	Sarah & Julie
9.00–11.00	paint front door	vacuum[1] carpets	——
11.00– 1.00	——	scrub floors	clean cupboards
2.00– 4.00	take curtains down	——	dust[2] furniture

[1] vacuum, *dt. staubsaugen*
[2] dust, *dt. abstauben*

1. .... Mr and Mrs Parker .... the front door by

   11 o'clock? – Yes, they .... it by 11 o'clock.

2. .... they .... the curtains down by 3 o'clock? –

   No, they .... them down until 4 o'clock.

3. .... Ben and Steve .... the carpets by 12 o'clock? –

   ....

4. .... they .... the floors by 12 o'clock? –

   .... them until 1 o'clock.

5. .... Sarah and Julie .... the cupboards by 12 o'clock? –

   ....

6. .... they .... the furniture by 6 o'clock ? –

   ....

Übung 3   Übersetze ins Englische.

1. Die Parkers werden den Frühjahrsputz (*engl. spring-cleaning*) bis 16 Uhr beendet haben.

   ....

   ....

2. Nächsten Monat werden die Parkers seit 20 Jahren hier wohnen.

   ....

3. Wird Mr Parker das Haus bis 8 Uhr verlassen haben?

   ....

11. Futurformen im Überblick

Futurform	Verwendung
will-Future	• für Vorhersagen und Vermutungen • für Angebote und Vorschläge (→ shall) • für spontane Entschlüsse • nach bestimmten Verben
going to-Future	• für feste Absichten und Pläne • für Ereignisse, für die es Anzeichen gibt
Simple Present	• für zukünftige Geschehen, die durch Zeit-pläne oder Programme festgelegt sind • in Nebensätzen der Zeit oder Bedingung
Present Progressive	• für Verabredungen und Pläne in der nahen Zukunft
Future Progressive	• für Handlungsabläufe in der Zukunft • für Zukunftspläne und zukünftige Geschehen • für höfliche Fragen (bzgl. der Zukunft)
Future Perfect	• für Ereignisse, die zu einem zukünftigen Zeitpunkt bereits vorbei sein werden

Übung 1

Bist du noch fit?
Bilde zu den Verben die angegebenen Futurformen.

buy	going to-Future	(bejaht) (Frage)	I .... you ....?
do	Future Perfect	(bejaht) (verneint)	he .... we ....
arrive	Simple Present	(Frage) (verneint)	.... it ....? it ....
lie	Future Progressive	(bejaht) (Frage)	she .... they ....?

rain	will-Future	(Frage) (verneint)	.... it .... ? it ....
stay	Present Progressive	(bejaht) (Frage)	I .... he .... ?

Übung 2

Als Futur-Profi könntest du die folgenden Situationen sicher auch auf Englisch meistern.
Welches ist die passende Futurform bei den unterstrichenen Sätzen? Kannst du deine Entscheidung begründen?

1. Beim Stadtbummel: „Das ist ja ein tolles T-Shirt! <u>Das kauf' ich mir!</u>"

   Futurform im Englischen: ....

   Begründung: ....

2. Am Bahnschalter: „<u>Wann fährt der nächste Zug nach Köln?</u>"

   Futurform im Englischen: ....

   Begründung: ....

3. Du träumst abends im Bett vor dich hin: „<u>Morgen um diese Zeit sitze ich im Zug.</u>"

   Futurform im Englischen: ....

   Begründung: ....

4. Du schaukelst in der Schule ganz wild auf deinem Stuhl.
   Dein Lehrer meint: „<u>Du wirst gleich runterfallen!</u>"

   Futurform im Englischen: ....

   Begründung: ....

5. Du bringst dein kaputtes Fahrrad zum Reparieren und fragst:
   „<u>Wann werden Sie das Rad repariert haben?</u>"

   Futurform im Englischen: ....

   Begründung: ....

6. Eine Freundin möchte wissen, was du morgen machst.
   Du sagst: „<u>Meine Cousine kommt morgen.</u>"

   Futurform im Englischen: ....

   Begründung: ....

12. Abschlusstest Futurformen

Übung 1   Morgen fahren Steve und Sarah mit ihrer Klasse nach Bath.
Sieh dir ihren Tagesablauf an und entscheide, welches Ereignis
gerade ablaufen oder bereits vorbei sein wird.

8.30 a.m.	leave Reading	1.00–2.00 p.m.	volleyball
8.30–10.00	train journey (dt. Zugfahrt)	2.30	go to the city centre
10.00	arrival at Bath	3.00–4.00	visit Roman baths
10.15–10.45	allocation (dt. Zuteilung) of rooms	4.00	coffee break
		4.30–5.30	Museum of Local Art
11.30–12.30	lunch	6.00	return to youth hostel

1. At 8.45 a.m. Steve and Sarah .... (leave) Reading.

   They .... (sit) in the train to Bath.

2. At 10.15 they .... (arrive) in Bath.

3. At 10.30 the allocation of the rooms .... (take place,
   dt. stattfinden).

4. At 12 o'clock everybody .... (have) lunch.

5. At 1.30 p.m. they .... (play) volleyball.

6. By 2.45 the class .... (go) to the city centre.

7. At 3.30 they .... (visit) the Roman baths.

8. At 4 o'clock they .... (have) a coffee break.

9. At 5 o'clock everybody .... (look) at the beautiful art
   objects in the Museum of Local Art.

10. By 6.30 the class .... (return) to the youth hostel.

Übung 2   Am Abend wird das Programm für den folgenden Tag
besprochen. – Hier kommen nun alle Futurformen vor!

Steve: What .... (we, do) tomorrow?

Mr Jackson: Well, tomorrow we .... (go) on a sightseeing tour first.

Emily: When .... (it, start)?

Mr Jackson: The tour .... (start) at 9 o'clock. Our bus ....
(leave) from in front of the youth hostel at half past eight and

.... (arrive) at the town hall (dt. Rathaus) at
eight-fifty.

Jenny: What do we have to take with us?

Mrs Leech:	I think you .... (need) an umbrella. I've just listened to the weather forecast. Tomorrow it .... (be) cloudy with some showers of rain.
Jenny:	Oh no! I have forgotten my umbrella!
Sarah:	No problem. I .... (lend) you one. I've got two, you know.
Sam:	When .... (tour, finish)?
Mr Jackson:	It .... (finish) at 11.30 a.m.
Donna:	What .... (do) afterwards?
Mrs Leech:	If you want to, you can spend the lunch-break together in groups of three or four.
Daniel:	Great! .... *(dt. Sollen wir)* have lunch at McDonald's?
Sam:	Good idea, Daniel! .... (you, eat) seven cheeseburgers again?
Daniel:	If I have enough time, I .... (be able) to eat eight or more.
Mr Jackson:	But don't forget to be back at the town hall at 1 p.m.
Sam:	We promise we .... (be) back on time. By this time Daniel .... (surely, finish) his eighth cheeseburger. – Sarah, what .... (you, do) at lunch time?
Sarah:	Well, Vicky and I have decided to spend the lunch-break at the river. At 12 o'clock we .... (sit) on a bench in the sunshine.
Sam:	But there .... (not, be) any sunshine tomorrow …
Sarah:	That's a pity. But I think Vicky and I .... (have) a nice break all the same. Without loads of cheeseburgers!

B If-Sätze

1. Grundlagen

Aufbau

If-Sätze bestehen aus zwei Teilen, nämlich

a) einem Nebensatz *(if-clause / if-Satz)* und

b) einem Hauptsatz *(main clause)*

(a) *If the weather is fine tomorrow,* (b) *we will go swimming.*

Bedingung und Folge

Im *if-*Satz wird eine Bedingung zum Ausdruck gebracht, im Hauptsatz steht die Folge aus dieser Bedingung:

<u>Bedingung</u>: (a) Wenn das Wetter morgen schön ist,

<u>Folge</u>: (b) gehen wir schwimmen.

Stellung und Kommasetzung

Steht der Nebensatz vor dem Hauptsatz, werden die beiden Satzteile durch ein Komma voneinander getrennt.

Der Hauptsatz kann aber auch vor dem *if-*Satz stehen; in diesem Fall wird kein Komma gesetzt:

(b) *We will go swimming* (a) *if the weather is fine tomorrow.*

Arten von Bedingungen

Die verschiedenen *if-*Satz-Typen im Englischen ergeben sich aus den unterschiedlichen Arten von Bedingungen:

1. wahrscheinliche oder erfüllte Bedingungen → *If it rains tomorrow, Steve and Eric will play computer games.*

2. unwahrscheinliche oder unmögliche Bedingungen → *If Ben had a lot of money, he would buy a car.*

3. nicht mehr erfüllbare Bedingungen → *If Steve had done his maths homework, his teacher wouldn't have been angry with him.*

Beachte:

Das deutsche „wenn" hat im Englischen unterschiedliche Entsprechungen:

1. *if* (dt. wenn, falls) gibt eine <u>Bedingung</u> an:
   If Sam meets Sarah, he'll invite her to his party.
   (→ Es ist nicht klar, ob Sam Sarah trifft.)

2. *when* (dt. wenn, sobald) nennt einen <u>Zeitpunkt</u>:
   When Sam meets Sarah, he'll invite her to his party.
   (→ Es steht bereits fest, dass Sam Sarah treffen wird.)

Übung 1   Welcher Satzteil stellt die Bedingung und welcher die Folge dar?

1. Mr Parker / win / in the lottery   he / buy / a car / for Ben

   Bedingung..   Folge..

2. Sarah / go / to Sam's party   he / invite / her

   ....

3. Mrs Parker / be / happy   Julie / help / her / with the housework

   ....

4. Steve / work / harder   he / get / a good mark

   ....

5. Julie and Jackie / not go / to the zoo   it / rain / tomorrow

   ....

6. The Parkers / go on holiday / to Spain   they / have / enough money

   ....

Übung 2   In welchen der folgenden if-Sätze muss ein Komma stehen? Setze es an die richtige Stelle.

1. If Mr Parker hurries he'll catch the train.
2. If I were you I would work harder.
3. We can go outside if it stops raining.
4. Can you answer the phone if it rings?
5. If Daniel hadn't eaten eight cheeseburgers he wouldn't have been sick afterwards.
6. Sarah would buy this skirt if it wasn't pink.
7. If you ever go to New York you must visit the *Museum of Modern Art*.
8. Ben would be really unhappy if he didn't pass his driving-test *(dt. Fahrprüfung)*.

Übung 3   Vervollständige die Sätze mit *if* bzw. *when*.

1. Sarah will take a hot shower .... she returns from Bath.

2. Laura will get the postcard next Wednesday .... Sarah posts it on Friday.

3. .... Steve were as old as Ben, he could take driving-lessons, too.

4. Ben: "I need more pocket money, Dad …"

   Mr Parker: "You'll get five pounds .... you mow the lawn *(dt. den Rasen*

   mähen)." Ben: "O.K., I'll do it .... I've finished my homework."

B 2. Typ I mit will-Future

Verwendung
- für (a) wahrscheinliche oder (b) erfüllte Bedingungen (→ Was ist, wenn …?)

→ *(a) If Ben passes his driving test, he'll give a big party.*
(b) If Eric likes tennis, he'll surely watch the match tonight.

Bildung:

Verb im *if*-Satz	Verb im Hauptsatz
Simple Present *If the sun comes out later,*	will-future *Steve and Eric will play tennis.*

Nicht vergessen:
Vollverben müssen im Simple Present mit *do* bzw. *does* verneint werden

→ *Mum will get very angry if you don't come immediately.*

Beachte:
Das Simple Present bezieht sich (a) auf die Zukunft bei erfüllbaren Bedingungen oder (b) auf die Gegenwart, wenn <u>gegenwärtig bestehende Zustände</u> ausgedrückt werden (erfüllte Bedingungen). Zustandsverben sind z. B. *be, believe, belong, cost, forget, have got, hate, like, love, remember, seem, understand, want, wish*

Übung 1   Verbinde die Satzhälften zu sinnvollen Sätzen.

1. If Steve doesn't hurry,
2. If you read through the text carefully,
3. Tom will join us at the cinema
4. My mother will be angry with me
5. If you help me with the maths homework,
6. I will return this book to Sue
7. If you bring some sandwiches,

a) I'll help you with the French translation.
b) if I don't help her with the housework.
c) I'll bring some cans of lemonade.
d) if I see her today.
e) he'll miss the bus.
f) you'll be able to answer the questions easily.
g) if you don't mind.

Übung 2   Sam möchte sich mal wieder mit Sarah verabreden.
Setze die richtigen Verbformen ein.

Sam: Hi, Sarah. What are you doing at the weekend?

Sarah: If the weather .... (be) nice, Vicky and I .... (go) shopping on Saturday.

Sam: And what .... (you, do) if the weather .... (not be) nice?

Sarah: We .... (probably, not stay) at home

even if it .... (not be) sunny. But if it ....

(rain), Vicky and I .... (meet) at my place and we

.... (prepare) our geography paper *(dt. Referat)* together.

Sam: Do you need some help?

Sarah: If you .... (be) keen on that stuff *(dt. Zeugs)*, we ....
(not send) you away.

Sam: What are you doing on Saturday evening? There's a good film at the *Odeon*.

Sarah: Well, my parents are spending a day in London on Saturday.

And Julie mustn't be left alone. But if they .... (return) in time,

I .... (be able) to join you.

Sam: And if they .... (not come back) in time?

Sarah: Hm … I've got an idea! If my parents .... (not return) in

time, we .... (watch) some videos. Is that okay with you?

Sam: Great! See you tomorrow …

Übung 3

Was machst du unter folgenden Bedingungen? – Bilde anhand der Stichpunkte englische Bedingungssätze vom Typ I.

1. weather / be / nice / tomorrow

If the weather .... nice tomorrow, I will ....

2. it / not rain / this afternoon

....

3. my friend X / visit / me / on Saturday

....

4. my parents / give / me / more pocket money / next month

....

....

B 3. Typ I mit Imperativ oder modalem Hilfsverb

Verwendung
s. Kap. B 2.

Bildung:

Verb im *if*-Satz	Verb im Hauptsatz
Simple Present *If it rains this afternoon,*	Imperativ *take an umbrella with you.*
Simple Present *If you don't have an umbrella,*	modales Hilfsverb + Grundform *you must stay indoors.* *you can stay indoors.* *you may stay indoors.*

Beachte:

I must ↔ I needn't	ich muss ↔ ich muss nicht
I may ↔ I mustn't	ich darf ↔ ich darf nicht

Übung 1   Verbinde die Satzhälften zu sinnvollen Sätzen.

1. If the water is too cold,
2. Julie must put on some weight
3. Steve can win the tennis trophy
4. If we don't hurry,
5. If you help me with the washing-up today,
6. You must do your homework on Sunday
7. If a stranger wants you to open the door,
8. Sarah can go to the cinema with Sam

a) you mustn't let him in.
b) if he is in good form tomorrow.
c) if Mr and Mrs Parker return in time.
d) you needn't help me tomorrow.
e) if you don't do it on Friday or Saturday.
f) we can't swim in the lake.
g) we won't see the beginning of the film.
h) if she weighs less than 20 kilos.

Übung 2   Sicher weißt du, welche Sehenswürdigkeiten man in welcher Stadt besichtigen kann (oder unbedingt muss). Bilde Sätze anhand der Vorgaben in der Tabelle.

Paris		visit	the *Ku'damm.*
Vienna	can	go to	the *Uffizien.*
London	must	walk along	the *Eiffel Tower.*
Berlin		see	*St Paul's Cathedral.*
Florence		have a look at	the *Hofburg.*

1. If you go to Paris, you ....

2. If you visit Vienna, ...

3. If you ....**.**

4. If ....**.**

5. ....**.**

Übung 3   Hier musst du nur noch die unterstrichenen Satzteile ins Englische übersetzen.

1. Wenn Julie in der Mathearbeit eine gute Note bekommt, <u>darf</u> sie in den Zoo <u>gehen</u>.

   If Julie gets a good mark in the maths test, she .... to the zoo.

2. Wenn Sarah heute nicht pünktlich zurück ist, <u>darf sie</u> morgen <u>nicht ausgehen</u>.

   If Sarah doesn't come back on time today, ... tomorrow.

3. Wenn Steve nicht um acht Uhr zurück ist, <u>kann er den Film nicht anschauen</u>.

   If Steve isn't back at 8 o'clock, ...**.**

4. Wenn Ben mehr Taschengeld will, <u>muss er seinem Vater im Garten helfen</u>.

   If Ben wants more pocket money, ...

   ....**.**

5. Wenn die Parkers eine Haushälterin einstellen, <u>braucht Frau Parker nicht die ganze Hausarbeit allein zu machen</u>.
   If the Parkers take on a housekeeper, ...

   ....**.**

Übung 4   Sarah hat aufgeschrieben, welche Sätze ihrer Eltern sie am meisten nerven. Übersetze sie ins Deutsche.

1. Don't forget your umbrella if it rains.

   ....

2. Tidy up your room if you don't find your things.

   ....

3. Help me with the housework if you don't have anything better to do.

   ....

   ....

4. Typ I: Mixed Exercises

Verb im *if*-Satz	Verb im Hauptsatz
Simple Present	a) *will*-Future oder b) modales Hilfsverb oder c) Imperativ
If the sun shines tomorrow,	a) *we will play in the garden.* b) *we can play in the garden.* c) *go and play in the garden.*

Übung 1

**Sarah möchte Laura in München besuchen.
Laura hat sich schon einiges überlegt.
Hilfst du ihr, den Brief ins Englische zu übersetzen?**

Liebe Sarah,
hast du dich schon entschieden, wann
du kommen möchtest?

Wenn du im August kommst, ist das
Wetter sicher schön.

Falls du an den Sehenswürdigkeiten
Münchens interessiert bist, können wir
eine Stadtführung machen.

Aber wir müssen (auch) keine machen,
wenn du das langweilig findest.

Wenn du gerne spazieren gehst, müssen
wir (unbedingt) zum *Englischen Garten*
gehen.

Falls du in München gerne Klamotten
kaufen willst, werde ich dir ein paar tolle
Geschäfte zeigen.

Ich bin mir sicher, dass wir zusammen
eine tolle Zeit haben werden.
Schreib bald!   Deine Laura

Dear Sarah,
Have you already decided when to
come?

If you .... in August, the

....

If .... interested in the sights

of Munich, we ....
a sight-seeing tour.

But we .... if

.... that's boring.

.... going for walks,

.... the
Englischer Garten.

....

clothes in Munich, ...
some fantastic shops.
I'm sure that we'll have a great time
together.
Write soon.   Love, Laura

Übung 2

Sam liegt abends in seinem Bett und plant das nächste *date* mit Sarah. – Setze die richtigen Verbformen ein.

1. If I .... (see) her tomorrow, I .... (ask) her whether she's got any plans for the weekend.

2. If she .... (not have) any plans, I .... (suggest, *dt. vorschlagen*) that we go on a cycling tour.

3. If she .... (not have) a bike, she .... (borrow, *können*) my sister's bike.

4. If she .... (not like) cycling, I .... (ask) her to go to the cinema with me.

5. If she .... (want) to go to the cinema, she .... (choose, *dürfen*) a film she would like to see.

6. If she .... (choose) a film I've already seen, I .... (not tell) her.

7. If she really .... (go) to the cinema with me, I .... (be) extremely happy.

Übung 3

Hier geht's nun um dich! Setze die fehlenden Bedingungen bzw. Folgen ein, so dass die Sätze auf dich zutreffen.

1. I'll be very happy if ....

2. If I get a good mark in my next English test, my parents ....
....

3. If my sister / brother uses my computer without asking me, I ....
....

4. I'll get very angry if ....

5. If it rains tomorrow, I ....

6. I'll be thankful *(dt. dankbar, froh)* if ....

B 5. Typ II mit unwahrscheinlicher Bedingung

Verwendung
- für Bedingungen, die unwahrscheinlich sind (→ Was würde geschehen, wenn …?)

→ *If Ben won a lot of money, he would buy a car.*

Bildung:

Verb im *if*-Satz	Verb im Hauptsatz
Simple Past	a) Conditional I: *would* + Grundform (Kurzform: *'d*) b) *could / might* + Grundform
If Mr Parker won in the lottery,	a) *he would buy a car for Ben.* b) *he could buy a car for Ben.*

Beachte:
Das Simple Past drückt hier keine Vergangenheit aus, sondern bezieht sich auf die Zukunft

→ *Steve would be sad if he lost the tennis match tomorrow.* (Es ist aber unwahrscheinlich, dass er es verlieren wird.)

Nicht vergessen:
Vollverben müssen im Simple Past mit *did* verneint werden

→ *Steve would be sad if he didn't win the tennis match tomorrow.*

Übung 1

**Bei den Parkers könnte einiges anders werden, wenn …
Setze die richtigen Verbformen ein.**

1. If Sarah .... (clean) her room more often, it .... (not look) such a mess.

2. Ben .... (get) more pocket money if he .... (help) his father more often in the garden.

3. If Steve .... (practise, *dt. trainieren*) even harder, he .... (become) the best tennis player in his school.

4. Julie .... (have) more time for painting pictures if she .... (not take) so many ballet classes.

Übung 2

Ben, Sarah, Steve und Julie spielen *Crazy Situations*.
In der Tabelle siehst du die gegebenen (unwahrscheinlichen)
Situationen sowie die verschiedenen Antworten. Bilde Sätze.

	Ben	Sarah	Steve	Julie
find a snake *(dt. Schlange)* in your bed	kill it	call the police	catch it	scream *(dt. schreien)*
meet an alien	say "hello"	ask its name	not do anything	be afraid

1. If Ben .... a snake in his bed, he .... it.

2. If Sarah .... a snake in her bed, she ....

3. If Steve .... a snake in his bed, ...

4. If Julie .... a snake in her bed, ...

5. If Ben .... an alien, he .... "hello".

6. If Sarah .... an alien, ...

7. If Steve ....

8. If Julie ....

Übung 3

Und was würdest du in diesen Situationen tun?
Vervollständige die Sätze und übersetze sie ins Deutsche.

1. If I .... (find) a snake in my bed, I ....

....

Wenn ich eine Schlange ....

....

2. If I .... (meet) an alien, I ....

Wenn ich einen Außerirdischen ....

....

B 6. Typ II mit unmöglicher Bedingung

Verwendung

- für Bedingungen, die unmöglich sind, weil sie den gegebenen Tatsachen widersprechen (→ Was wäre, wenn ...?)

→ *If Ben had a lot of money, he would buy a car.*
(Er hat aber nicht viel Geld!)

Bildung:

Verb im *if*-Satz	Verb im Hauptsatz
Simple Past	*would / could / might* + Grundform

Beachte:

Das Simple Past drückt hier keine Vergangenheit aus, sondern bezieht sich auf die Gegenwart

→ *If I had enough money, I would buy this T-shirt.*
(Wenn ich (jetzt) genug Geld hätte ...)

Um jemandem einen Rat zu geben, kann man den Ausdruck *If I were you ...* verwenden

→ *If I were you, I wouldn't buy these shoes.*
(Wenn ich du wäre ... / Ich an deiner Stelle ...)

Übung 1

Sarah ist heute mal wieder total unzufrieden mit sich selbst und wünscht sich, dass vieles anders wäre.
Setze die richtigen Verbformen ein.
Beachte die Stellung von Bedingung und Folge.

1. If I .... (have) dark hair, I .... (look) much better.

2. If I .... (not have) such short legs, I .... (wear) mini-skirts.

3. I .... (be) much happier if my hair .... (not be) so curly.

4. If I .... (be) taller, I .... (wear) these fashionable trousers.

5. I .... (not be) so self-conscious (*dt. befangen*) if I ....

.... (not have) so many spots (*dt. Pickel*).

Übung 2   Steve hat sich in Lucy verliebt und würde sie gerne anrufen, weiß aber ihre Nummer nicht. Er träumt vor sich hin …

1. I / know / Lucy's number, I / phone / her

   If I .... Lucy's number, I .... her.

2. she / not / be / so beautiful, I / dare (dt. sich etw. trauen) to tell / her / I love her

   If ....

3. she / be / my girl-friend, I / be / the happiest person in the world

   ....

4. I / have / lots of money, I / buy / her / anything she wants

   ....

Übung 3   Freunde von dir wollen in den folgenden Situationen deinen Rat. Verwende die gegebenen Stichwörter.

1. Friend A: "I look a mess. What shall I do with my hair?" (go / hairdresser's)

   You: "If I .... you, I ...."

2. Friend B: "I lied to my mother. I feel terrible." (tell / her / truth)

   You: "If I ...."

3. Friend C: "I've put on weight (put on weight, dt. zunehmen)." (do / a lot of sport)

   You: "If ...."

4. Friend D: "These trousers look great. But they're too small." (not / buy / them)

   You: ....

Übung 4   Vollende die angefangenen Sätze in deinem Sinne und übersetze sie ins Deutsche.

1. If I were eighteen, I ....

   ....

2. If I were a pop star, ...

   ....

3. If I had lots of money, ...

   ....

7. Typ I und Typ II im Vergleich

Typ I	Typ II
Verwendung	
• für wahrscheinliche oder erfüllte Bedingungen	• für unwahrscheinliche oder unmögliche Bedingungen

Bildung:

if-Satz	Hauptsatz
Simple Present	will-Future modales Hilfsverb Imperativ

if-Satz	Hauptsatz
Simple Past	would / could / might + Grundform

If it rains, Sarah and Sam will watch some videos.
(Auf Grund des Wetterberichts ist mit Regen zu rechnen.)

↔ *If it didn't rain, Sarah and Sam would go swimming.*
(Es ist unwahrscheinlich, dass es nicht regnet.)

If it's cold outside, you can't wear shorts.
(Heute ist es kalt draußen.)

↔ *If it wasn't so cold now, Sarah could wear shorts.*
(Jetzt ist es aber kalt.)

Übung 1   Trage die folgenden if-Sätze in die richtige Spalte der Tabelle ein.

a) Steve and Eric can play tennis if the sun comes out later.
b) If I were you, I wouldn't tell her secrets any more.
c) If the sun shines, we won't stay indoors.
d) What would you do if you met the Queen in the street?
e) If Ben had enough time today, he could help his father in the garden.
f) Tidy up your room if you don't know what else to do.

Typ I	Typ II

Übung 2

Handelt es sich bei den folgenden if-Sätzen um Typ I oder Typ II? Setze die fehlende Verbform ein.

1. If my grandma .... (give) me some money, I can buy a new skateboard.

2. Sarah .... (phone) Laura more often if it was cheaper.

3. If you help me with the washing-up, I .... (clean) your shoes.

4. If I .... (be) you, I would tell my parents the truth.

5. Would you mind if I .... (open) the window?

6. .... (go) to your room if you keep on shouting like this.

Übung 3

**Lies dir die folgenden Situationen durch und entscheide, ob die Bedingung erfüllbar ist oder nicht.
Setze dann die richtigen Verbformen ein.**

1. *Steve is alone in his room. He is thinking ...*

   a) If Eric .... (be) here now, we .... (play) tennis.

   b) If he .... (come) later, we .... (play) tennis.

2. *Sarah and Vicky are in a shop. Sarah is trying on (try on, dt. anprobieren) a blue dress. She says:*

   a) "I .... (love) to buy this dress if it .... (be) red."

   b) "If I .... (find) a red one in another shop, I .... (buy) it."

3. *It is a warm, sunny day. Ben and Emma are sitting in the garden. Ben is thinking ...*

   a) We .... (go) inside if it .... (get) colder later.

   b) If it .... (not be) sunny, we .... (not spend) the day in the garden.

4. *Julie's classmates often laugh at her and call her "little baby", because she still takes her doll to school.*

   a) If Julie .... (not take) her doll to school, they .... (not call) her "little baby".

   b) If she .... (leave) it at home next week, they .... (not laugh) at her any more.

B 8. Typ III

Verwendung

- für Bedingungen, die in der Vergangenheit nicht gegeben waren, also <u>nicht mehr</u> erfüllbar sind (→ Was wäre gewesen, wenn …?)

→ *If Ben had made one more mistake, he wouldn't have passed the driving-test.* (Er hat aber keinen weiteren Fehler mehr gemacht!)

Bildung:

Verb im *if*-Satz	Verb im Hauptsatz
Past Perfect	a) Conditional II: *would + have + 3. Form* b) *could / might + have +* 3. Form
If Steve had known Lucy's phone number, (Er wusste sie aber nicht!)	a) *he would have phoned her.* b) *he could have asked her to visit him.*

Beachte:

Die Kurzform *'d* steht

- im if-Satz für *had*
- im Hauptsatz für *would*

→ *If I'd known your number,*
→ *I'd have called you.*

Merke

Signalwörter

Zeitangaben der Vergangenheit, z. B. *yesterday, last (week)* …

Übung 1

Steht *'d* hier für *had* oder für *would*?
Schreibe die volle Form hinter die Kurzform.

1. If Ben had had enough time, he'd have helped = ... his father in the garden.

2. Sarah wouldn't have gone to the cinema if she'd known = ... that it was such a bad film.

3. If he'd felt = ... better, Steve would have won the tennis match.

4. We'd have gone = ... to

   the theatre if we'd had = ... enough money.

Übung 2
Steve kommt nach seinem verlorenen Spiel nach Hause. Setze die richtigen Verbformen ein.

Mrs Parker: Hi, Steve. How was the match?

Steve: It was awful, Mum. I lost.

Mrs Parker: Never mind, Steve. But what happened?

Steve: It was just too hot. If it .... (not be) so hot,

I .... (win) the match.

Mrs Parker: Why is that?

Steve: My hands were wet with sweat. If I ....

(not sweat) so much, I .... (hit) more balls.

Mrs Parker: Did you have enough mineral water with you?

Steve: No, just one bottle. If I .... (take) more water with me,

I .... (not get) tired so quickly.

And to make things worse I even forgot my sunglasses.

I'm sure I .... (play) much better

if I .... (not forget) my sunglasses.

Mrs Parker: Don't blame it on the sunglasses, Steve. You just had a bad day.

Steve: You're probably right, Mum. If I .... (be) in form,

I .... (not lose) the match.

Übung 3
Auch Sarah hatte einen schlechten Tag und überlegt, was anders sein hätte können, wenn … – Bilde if-Sätze vom Typ III.

1. I went to bed late last night. That's why I overslept (oversleep, *dt. verschlafen*).

   If I .... to bed earlier, I ....

2. I was hungry all morning, because I didn't have time for breakfast.

   I wouldn't ....

   ....

3. I didn't study enough for the maths test. I couldn't answer all the questions.

   ....

   ....

9. Unmögliche Bedingungen im Vergleich (Typ II und Typ III)

Typ II	Typ III

Verwendung

- für Bedingungen, die unmöglich sind, weil sie in der Gegenwart nicht erfüllt werden können
- für Bedingungen, die unmöglich sind, weil sie in der Vergangenheit nicht erfüllt wurden

Bildung:

if-Satz	Hauptsatz
Simple Past	would / could / might + Grundform

if-Satz	Hauptsatz
Past Perfect	would / could / might + have + 3. Form

If the weather was nice, we would play outdoors.
(Es ist aber nicht schön!)

↔

If the weather had been nice, we would have played outdoors.
(Es war aber nicht schön!)

Merke

Signalwörter:

Typ II
Zeitangaben der Gegenwart, z. B. *today, now*

↔

Typ III
Zeitangaben der Vergangenheit, z. B. *last (year), yesterday, (two days) ago*

Übung 1

Die folgenden Satzpaare sind nur auf den ersten Blick ähnlich. Handelt es sich um *if*-Sätze des Typs II oder III? Setze die richtige Verbform ein.

1. If Sam had enough money, he _____ (buy) a bunch of flowers for Sarah.

2. If Sam had had enough money last week, he _____ (buy) a bottle of perfume for Sarah.

3. Ben would be sad if Emma _____ (not be) here now.

4. Ben would have been sad if he _____ (not pass) his driving-test.

5. Julie _____ (paint) some pictures if it had rained yesterday.

6. Julie _____ (not sit) in the garden if it was raining now.

Übung 2   Forme die folgenden Sätze in *if*-Sätze vom Typ II bzw. III um.

1. Julie can't draw now because she can't find her pencil.

   If Julie .... her pencil, she .... now.

2. Steve didn't play tennis yesterday because his right leg hurt.

   Steve .... tennis yesterday if ....

   ....

3. Ben doesn't see Emma very often these days because he has such a lot of homework to do.

   ....

   ....

4. Sarah couldn't bake a cake last Sunday because she forgot to buy some eggs.

   ....

   ....

Übung 3   Laura geht seit drei Wochen mit Jonas.
In einem Brief will sie Sarah von ihrem ersten Streit berichten.
Hilfst du ihr beim Übersetzen?

… Wenn ich gestern nicht zu Hause gewesen wäre, hätte er mich (gar) nicht besuchen können. Wenn wir uns nicht getroffen hätten, hätten wir nicht gestritten (streiten, *engl. argue*).

Vielleicht wäre er nicht gegangen, wenn ich ihm zugehört hätte.

Jetzt bin ich total unglücklich.

Was würdest du an meiner Stelle tun? Ich wäre so glücklich, wenn er jetzt hier wäre …

If I .... at home

yesterday, he ....

me. If ...., we

....

He ....

if I ....

I'm extremely unhappy now.

What ....

....

....

10. Typ I, Typ II und Typ III im Vergleich

Verwendung:
Folgende Tabelle zeigt dir den Zusammenhang zwischen Art der Bedingung und zeitlichem Bezug der Bedingung.

	Zukunft	Gegenwart	Vergangenheit
Typ I	wahrscheinlich	erfüllt	——
Typ II	unwahrscheinlich	unmöglich	——
Typ III	——	——	nicht mehr möglich

Beachte:
Bezieht sich eine Bedingung auf die Zukunft oder Gegenwart, musst du oft aus dem Textzusammenhang erschließen, ob du Typ I oder Typ II verwenden musst.

Bildung:

Typ I	*if*-Satz	Simple Present
	Hauptsatz	will-Future / modales Hilfsverb / Imperativ
Typ II	*if*-Satz	Simple Past
	Hauptsatz	*would / could / might* + Grundform
Typ III	*if*-Satz	Past Perfect
	Hauptsatz	*would / could / might + have* + 3. Form

Typ I	If it is warm tomorrow, Sarah and Vicky will go swimming.
Typ II	If it was warm now, Sarah and Vicky would spend the afternoon in the garden.
Typ III	If it had been warm yesterday, Sarah and Vicky would have done a cycling tour.

Handschriftliche Notizen:
1) Gegenwart (if)
   → Futur I
2) Vergangenheit 1 (if)
   → konditional 1
3) 3 Verg. (if).
   → Konditional 2

Konditional
→ Möglichkeits-
   form

Übung 1   Stelle bei den folgenden if-Sätzen den Satztyp fest.

1. If Julie found a purse in the street, she'd take it to the police. → Typ II

2. Mr Parker will miss the train if he doesn't hurry. → Typ I

3. Steve might have won the match if he had been in form. → Typ III

4. If Ben has got enough money, he'll give a big party next week. → Typ I

5. If Sarah hadn't forgotten her textbook at school, she would have been able to do her homework. → Typ III

Übung 2

Bestimme bei den folgenden Sätzen den zeitlichen Bezug, die Art der Bedingung und somit den Typ I, II oder III.
Achte bei der Übersetzung insbesondere auf die Verbformen und die Stellung von Haupt- und Nebensatz.

1. Wenn Sarah zu Hause gewesen wäre, hätte Sam sie ins Kino eingeladen.

   zeitl. Bezug: .... Bedingung: .... Typ ....

   Übersetzung: If Sarah ....

   ....

2. *Der Wetterbericht hat für morgen schönes Wetter und Temperaturen bis zu 27°C vorher-gesagt.*
   Wenn es morgen regnen würde, könnten Sarah und Sam kein Picknick machen (ein Picknick machen, *engl. to have a picnic*).

   zeitl. Bezug: .... Bedingung: .... Typ ....

   Übersetzung: ....

   ....

3. Sarah wird ihre neuen Shorts anziehen, falls es morgen richtig heiß wird.

   zeitl. Bezug: .... Bedingung: .... Typ ....

   Übersetzung: ....

   ....

4. Wenn Sam gerne schwimmt, kann er im See ein Bad nehmen *(engl. have a swim)*.

   zeitl. Bezug: .... Bedingung: .... Typ ....

   Übersetzung: ....

   ....

5. *Bevor Sam und Sarah am nächsten Tag losziehen, sagt Mrs Parker zu Sarah:*
   „Ich an deiner Stelle (= Wenn ich du wäre) würde ein Insektenschutzmittel *(engl. insect repellent)* mitnehmen."

   zeitl. Bezug: .... Bedingung: .... Typ ....

   Übersetzung: ....

   ....

If-Sätze

Übung 1

Lies dir die folgenden if-Sätze durch und entscheide, welche der beiden Aussagen jeweils zutrifft. Kreuze an!

1. Ben wouldn't go to school by motor-bike if it rained tomorrow. → ○ es ist wahrscheinlich, dass es regnet
   ○ es ist unwahrscheinlich, dass es regnet
2. If Jenny comes to Ben's party, she'll bring a chocolate cake. → ○ mit Jennys Kommen ist zu rechnen
   ○ mit Jennys Kommen ist nicht zu rechnen
3. Sarah wouldn't have got a bad mark if she had worked harder. → ○ Sarah hat zu wenig für die Schule getan
   ○ Sarah tut momentan zu wenig
4. If Vicky had known that Sarah was at home, she would have visited her. → ○ Vicky wusste, dass Sarah zu Hause ist
   ○ Vicky wusste nicht, dass Sarah zu Hause ist
5. Mr Parker could drive Julie to the pool if he was back at 4 p.m. → ○ er wird um 16 Uhr wahrscheinlich zurück sein
   ○ er wird um 16 Uhr wohl nicht zurück sein

Übung 2

Als Sarah Lauras Brief erhält, ruft sie sie sofort an, um zu erfahren, ob Laura und Jonas sich wieder versöhnt haben.
Setze die richtigen Verbformen ein.

Sarah: Hi, Laura. How are you?

Laura: Hi, Sarah. Not too good. Are you in a hurry?

Sarah: Of course I'm not. I .... (not phone) you if I

.... (not have) time. Why are you asking?

Laura: Well, it's quite a long story … Jonas and I had another argument (dt. Streit).

Sarah: Oh dear! What happened?

Laura: I was playing games on Jonas' computer when it suddenly crashed. I really felt

sorry. If it .... (not be) me who was playing,

it .... (not be) my fault (dt. Fehler).

Sarah: I don't think that's such a big problem. What did Jonas do then?

Laura: He called me a fool. Then I went mad and threw some CDs at him.

You know, I .... (not throw) CDs

at him if he .... (not call) me a fool.

Sarah: Did they hit him?

Laura: No, the CDs missed him and landed on his bed. I think I ....

(feel) sorry if I .... (hurt) him.

Sarah: What did you do then?

Laura: I left at once. And Jonas didn't stop me going.

Sarah: Have you heard anything from him since?

Laura: No, not yet. And I'm sure that he won't phone me. If he .... (phone) and .... (say) he was sorry that he'd called me a fool, everything .... (be) all right again. But I think it's over. What .... (you, do) if you .... (be) me?

Sarah: Well, I think it's not just his fault. If I .... (be) you, I .... (call) him and ask him to forgive me as well.

Laura: Maybe you're right, Sarah. If he .... (not call) me within the next few hours, I .... (call) him. – Just a second, Sarah. The doorbell is ringing. If it .... (be) Jonas, I .... (tell) him that I'm really sorry and that I still love him ...

Übung 3

Auch Sarah hat ein Problem: ihre verpatzte Matheschulaufgabe. Kannst du ihren Tagebucheintrag übersetzen?

May 26

I've got a 'D' *(dt. Note 4)* in the maths test. Ugh! If I had worked harder I wouldn't have got such a bad mark. And I might have done better if Mr Summer had explained the subject *(dt. Stoff)* properly *(dt. richtig, anständig)*. Sam said "I wouldn't worry if I were you. You've got enough good marks." Maybe he's right. If I don't get another 'D', there'll be a 'B' *(dt. Note 2)* in my report *(dt. Zeugnis)*.

26. Mai

12. Sonderformen

Neben den bisher aufgeführten Haupttypen der if-Sätze gibt es – abhängig von Art der Bedingung und zeitlichem Bezug – diverse Sonderformen.

Folgende Varianten <u>können</u> (je nach Bundesland, Schulart und Lehrbuch), müssen aber nicht, Stoff der 7. oder 8. Klasse sein. Abweichungen gegenüber den Haupttypen sind unterstrichen.

Typ I

	if-Satz	Hauptsatz
• wenn die Bedingung bereits erfüllt worden ist	<u>Present Perfect</u>	will-Future modales Hilfsverb Imperativ

→ *If you've been to Rome, you can tell me something about its sights.*

• bei bestehenden Fähigkeiten (→ *can*) oder Verpflichtungen (→ *must*)	<u>modales Hilfsverb</u> (bzw. zugehörige Ersatzverben)	will-Future modales Hilfsverb Imperativ

→ *If you can speak English, you'll be able to translate this.*

• wenn der Verlauf einer Bedingung betont wird	<u>Present Progressive*</u>	will-Future modales Hilfsverb Imperativ

→ *If it's raining, Julie will stay indoors.*   * <u>nur bei Tätigkeitsverben!</u>

• wenn eine logische Folge ausgedrückt wird	Simple Present	<u>Simple Present</u>

→ *If you put ice into a hot oven, it melts* (*melt*, dt. schmelzen).

Typ II

• für eine bestehende (irreale) Bedingung mit Folgen für die Vergangenheit	Simple Past	*<u>would / could / might + have + 3. Form</u>*

→ *If Vicky's parents had more money, they would have spent their holiday at the seaside.*

Typ III

• für eine (irreale) Bedingung in der Vergangenheit mit Folgen für die Gegenwart	Past Perfect	*<u>would / could / might + Grundform</u>*

→ *If Sarah hadn't spent all her money, she could buy that CD now.*

Übung 1   Ordne den Sätzen die jeweilige Begründung zu.

1. If you mix red and blue, you get purple.
2. If Julie has finished her homework, she may visit Jackie.
3. Laura would be sad if she hadn't made it up (make it up, *dt. sich versöhnen*) with Jonas.
4. If you have to learn your vocabulary, you needn't help me with the washing-up.
5. Sam would have bought lots of presents for Sarah's birthday if he was rich.
6. Don't disturb Dad if he's working.

a) Bedingung ist im Verlauf
b) Bedingung liegt in der Vergangenheit, die Folge in der Gegenwart
c) Verpflichtung in der Gegenwart
d) Bedingung liegt in der Gegenwart, die Folge in der Vergangenheit
e) logische Folge
f) Bedingung ist bereits erfüllt worden

Übung 2   Überlege, welche Art von Bedingung jeweils gegeben ist und setze dann die richtige Verbform ein.

1. Don't interrupt Mum if she .... (still, talk) on the phone.

2. If there's no battery in your personal stereo, it .... (not work).

3. Mr Parker .... (not be) angry with Sarah now if she hadn't been so lazy.

4. Steve may watch TV if he .... (already, clean) his room.

5. If Vicky's mother .... (speak, *können*) two foreign languages, she'll get the job.

6. If the Parkers had lots of money, they .... (fly) to Australia last year.

Übung 3   Gleich hast du's geschafft! – Übersetze ins Englische.

1. Wenn man zu viel Fastfood isst, wird man dick.

....

2. Julie wäre jetzt nicht krank, wenn sie gestern wärmere Kleidung getragen hätte.

....

....

3. Wenn du diese Sätze richtig übersetzt hast, darfst du dich Profi (*engl. pro*) nennen.

....

....

Englisch

7./8. Klasse

Verena Rotter

If-Sätze und Futurformen

Lösungsteil
(an der Perforation heraustrennen)

Mentor Übungsbuch 855

Mentor Verlag München

A Futurformen
1. Will-Future für Vermutungen und Vorhersagen

> Beim will-Future *kannst du im bejahten oder verneinten Satz entweder die Langform*
> (will / will not) *oder die Kurzform* ('ll / won't) *verwenden. Beides ist richtig.*
> *Der besseren Übersichtlichkeit halber findest du in der Regel im Folgenden nur eine Form.*
> *Im mündlichen Sprachgebrauch sind Kurzformen generell üblicher.*

Übung 1
Tomorrow it'll be / will be warm and sunny in South England.
There will be light winds from the South-West only.
The Midlands will be cloudy, but it will stay dry.
It will rain heavily in Scotland tomorrow.
In the Highlands there will be strong winds from the North-West and the temperature
there will not go / won't go above 8°C.
In Wales it will be cloudy, but it won't rain all day.
You will even have some sunny spells in the early evening.
Beachte, dass even *zwischen dem Hilfsverb* (will) *und dem Vollverb* (have) *steht.*
In Northern Ireland it will be cloudy with lots of rain.
Temperatures won't climb above 10°C.

Übung 2
I will earn lots of money.
I will have a husband and (some) children.
I will have to cook dinner for my family.
Zur Erinnerung: have to *ist das Ersatzverb zu* must.
I won't have to be at home at 8 p.m.
I won't go to bed at 10 p.m.
My parents will be over 60.

Übung 3
1. Will I fall in love soon? / Will I soon fall in love?
2. Will I get good marks?
3. Will Petra really move away from Munich?
4. Will I get a snowboard for my birthday?
Beachte die Präposition for.
Nicht vergessen:
bekommen heißt auf Englisch get *oder* receive, *das englische* become *heißt werden!*

2. Will-Future für spontane Entschlüsse und Angebote

Übung 1

1. Sarah: "I'll do the washing-up for you, Mum."
2. Julie: "No problem, Mum, I'll go and buy some."
3. Ben & Steve: "We'll buy a new bottle for you."
4. Sarah & Steve: "We'll stay at home and we'll sit at her bedside all night, Mum."

Muttertag wird in Großbritannien übrigens im März gefeiert!

Übung 2

Das will-Future *kannst du im Deutschen entweder mit dem Futur I oder mit der Gegenwart wiedergeben.*

1. Ich verspreche (euch), dass wir um 11 Uhr / 23 Uhr zurückkommen / zurückkommen werden.
2. Ich hoffe, dass es keinen Stau gibt / geben wird.
   oder freier: ... dass wir nicht im Stau stecken (werden).
3. Ich nehme an / denke, dass Julies Temperatur / Fieber nicht weiter ansteigt / ansteigen wird.
   Nicht vergessen: der Genitiv (hier: Julies) wird im Deutschen ohne *Apostroph gebildet*
4. Ich rechne damit / denke / glaube, dass Julie bald einschläft / einschlafen wird.

Wenn deine Version der Übersetzung nicht genau mit den hier aufgeführten Lösungsvorschlägen übereinstimmt, heißt das nicht, dass sie falsch ist.
Zieh am besten ein Lexikon zu Rate, falls du dir nicht sicher bist.

Übung 3

1. Julie: "I'm so bored. What shall we do tonight / this evening?"
2. Sarah: "Shall I get you / fetch you a cup of tea?"
3. Steve: "Shall I turn the TV on?"
4. Sarah & Steve: "Shall we read you a story?"
5. Steve: "Shall I bring your colouring book?"

Übung 4

1. + d) Shall we go to the cinema tonight? → Vorschlag
2. + e) I wonder what the film will be like. → will-Future nach bestimmten Verben
3. + a) There will be seven billion people on our planet soon. → Vorhersage
4. + c) A: I like this sweater. – B: I'll buy it for you. → spontanes Angebot
5. + b) I think Sarah will get a good mark in her German test. → Vermutung

3. Going to-Future

> *Beim* going to-Future *kannst du die Formen von* to be *als Langform (am / are / is) oder als Kurzform ('m / 're / 's) verwenden. Im mündlichen Sprachgebrauch sind Kurzformen üblicher.*

Übung 1

Mrs Parker: Steve, have you done the shopping yet?
Steve: Not yet, Mum. I'm going to do it later.
Mrs Parker: Sarah, have you cleaned the rooms yet?
Sarah: I've cleaned Ben and Steve's room as well as mine. But Julie's room looks such a mess. I'm not going to clean it.
Mrs Parker: I've just talked to her. She's going to clean the room herself.
Sarah: Has she got time to do it? It's her turn to scrub the kitchen floor, isn't it?
Mrs Parker: You are right, Sarah. It *is* her turn, but she isn't going to scrub the floor. She said she's still too ill …

Übung 2

1. Julie has put milk onto the stove. She forgets to turn the hot-plate off. The milk is going to boil over.
2. Steve and Eric are climbing up an old ladder to pick apples. One rung of the ladder is loose. They are going to fall off the ladder.
3. Sarah is running a bath. She leaves the bathroom and talks to her friend Vicky on the phone for an hour. The water is going to flood the whole house.
4. Ben is driving a car without a driver's licence. He hasn't slept for 24 hours. He is going to have an accident.

Übung 3

Dear Sarah,
You wrote in your last letter that you are going to give a big party together with Steve …
Where are you going to celebrate?
Who are you going to invite?
What kind of music are you going to play?
Is your mother going to make her delicious salads again?
What are you going to give Steve for his birthday?
I wish I could celebrate with you.
Yours, Laura

4. Will-Future und going to-Future im Vergleich

Übung 1

Diese Übung behandelt (feste) Pläne. Deshalb musst du hier das going to-Future *verwenden. Es bleibt dir überlassen, wie viele Sätze du mit* I, my parents, my sister / brother *(falls du Geschwister hast) oder* my friend *bildest.*
Folgende Lösungen sind nur Vorschläge!
Achte auf die richtige Form von to be.

1. I'm going to watch TV tonight.
2. My parents are going to visit my grandparents next weekend.
3. My sister is going to play tennis tonight.
4. My friend is going to visit me next weekend.
5. I'm going to read the latest novel of my favourite writer in the holidays.
6. My brother is going to learn to sail in the holidays.
7. My sister is going to give a party next weekend.

Übung 2

Bei spontanen Angeboten, wie sie in dieser Übung vorkommen, musst du das will-Future *verwenden.*

1. Sarah: "We haven't got enough biscuits."
   Vicky: "I'll bake some."
2. Steve: "We've only got fifteen CDs."
   Joe: "I'll bring my CD collection."
3. Sarah: "Oh no! I've dropped the chocolate cake!"
   Karen & Amy: "Never mind. We'll make a new one."
4. Steve: "Look! We've only got twenty glasses. We need another ten or twelve."
   Susan: "No problem. I'll go and get you twenty if you like."

Übung 3

1. Karen: "Vicky, do you think Sarah will like our present?"
   Mit think *wird eine Vermutung zum Ausdruck gebracht* → will-Future
2. Vicky: "I'm sure she'll love it."
   Nach der Wendung I'm sure *verwendet man ebenfalls das* will-Future.
3. Eric: "What are you going to give Steve?"
   Eric geht davon aus, dass Justin schon weiß, was er Steve schenken wird (und es sich nicht um eine spontane Idee handelt) → going to-Future
4. Justin: "I'm going to give him a poster of Andre Agassi."
   Justin hat sich schon ein Geschenk überlegt (oder bereits gekauft) → going to-Future
5. Justin: "I suppose Steve will put it onto the wall."
   Suppose gehört zu den in die Zukunft weisenden Verben, nach denen das will-Future *steht.*

5. Will-Future und going to-Future: Mixed Exercises

Übung 1

Für Vorschläge und Angebote („ Soll ich …?" / „ Sollen wir …?") verwendet man shall.
1. Mrs Parker: "Shall I open a window / the window / the windows?"
2. Mr Parker: "Shall I get you a chair?"
3. Mr & Mrs Parker: "Shall we go and get some more?"
4. Mr Parker: "Shall I play one of my Beatles cassettes?"
5. Mrs Parker: "Shall I drive you home?"
6. Mrs Parker: "Shall I make the guest bed for her?"

Übung 2

Grandma: Well, Steve and Sarah, what are you going to do with the money (…)?
Grandma fragt nach den Plänen, die Sarah mit dem Geld hat → going to-Future

Sarah: I've already decided that I'm going to save half of it.
Sarahs Absicht, die Hälfte zu sparen besteht schon länger → going to-Future

Grandma: And what about the other half?

Sarah: I haven't had the time to spend it yet, but I'm definitely going to buy the brand new *Spice Girls* CD.
Auch hier handelt es sich um eine feste, wohl überlegte Absicht
Beachte die Stellung von definitely!

Grandma: And what are you going to do with the rest?

Sarah: I'm going to give Mum and Dad tickets for the theatre because they helped us so much with our party.
Feste Pläne → going to-Future

Grandma: That's very nice of you, Sarah. And what are you going to do with the money, Steve?

Steve: Well, unlike Sarah, I'm certainly not going to save any of it.
Es ist Steves fester Entschluss nichts zu sparen → going to-Future
Beachte die Stellung von certainly!

Grandma: What are you going to buy then?

Steve: I haven't thought about it so far. Perhaps I'll buy a pair of new tennis shoes.
Durch perhaps *wird eine Vermutung ausgedrückt → will-Future*

Grandma: I hope I'll find nice ones.
Hope gehört zu den Verben, die in die Zukunft weisen → will-Future

Steve: And tomorrow I'm going to do a cycling tour with James and Eric.
Die Radtour ist bereits fest geplant → going to-Future
I'm sure I'll need some money.
Signalwort: I'm sure → will-Future

Grandma: Have you listened to the weather forecast?

Steve: Yes, I have. It will be cloudy but it won't rain.
Bei Wettervorhersagen steht das will-Future.

Übung 3

1. It will be rather cold tomorrow. → Vorhersage → will
2. Shall we go swimming? → Vorschlag → shall
3. I'm going to watch a video tonight. → Plan, feste Absicht → going to
4. I promise I'll be back in 5 minutes. → nach einem Verb, das in die Zukunft weist → will
5. Look at the sky. It's going to rain. → absehbares Ereignis → going to
6. I think Ben will pass the test easily. → Vermutung → will
7. (A: I'm too tired to do the shopping.) → Spontanes Angebot → will
B: No problem. I'll do it for you.

6. Simple Present mit zukünftiger Bedeutung

Übung 1

Steve: Excuse me, Mr Hill, when does the next bus to the city centre leave?

Mr Hill: It leaves in about ten minutes. What are you going to visit?

Eric: Well, first of all we'd like to go on a sight-seeing tour. Do you know where the tours start?

Mr Hill: They start in front of the town hall on the hour.

Steve: And I'd like to go to the *British Handcraft Museum*.

Mr Hill: You'll have to hurry then, boys. The museum closes at 4 o'clock.

Eric: And when does it open tomorrow morning? Just in case we don't manage to get there in time ...

Mr Hill: I think it opens at 9 a.m. I can check that for you.
Why don't you go to the inline-disco tonight?

James: Inline-disco? Great! Where does it take place and when does it begin?

Mr Hill: It's in the sports centre in Beechwood Road. And it starts at 8 p.m. and finishes at 11 p.m. But don't forget that the youth hostel closes at 10.30 p.m.

Hast du an das -s bei der 3. Person Singular (he, she, it) gedacht?
Nicht vergessen: nach o, s, x, z, ch und sh (wie hier bei finish) *musst du -es anhängen.*

Übung 2

Bei der folgenden Übung kann in der Regel der Nebensatz vor oder nach dem Hauptsatz stehen.
Beachte, dass das Verb im Hauptsatz im will-Future *und das im Nebensatz im* Simple Present *stehen muss.*

1. Steve will go to bed as soon as he returns from the cyclingtour.
   oder As soon as Steve returns from the cyclingtour, he will go to bed.
2. Sarah will take a shower before she goes to the cinema.
   oder Before Sarah goes to the cinema she will take a shower.
3. Mr Parker will phone his wife when he arrives in Birmingham.
   oder When Mr Parker arrives in Birmingham he will phone his wife.
4. The children won't start breakfast until their parents sit down at the table.

Bei der Wendung not ... until *ist ein einfaches Umstellen von Haupt- und Nebensatz nicht möglich. Will man hier den Nebensatz vor den Hauptsatz stellen, hat dies eine so genannte Inversion zur Folge:*
Not until their parents arrive will the children start breakfast.
Grammatikalische Strukturen dieser Art gehören jedoch nicht zum Stoffgebiet der 7. und 8. Jahrgangsstufe.

7. Present Progressive mit zukünftiger Bedeutung

Übung 1

1. Mr Parker is going to the dentist on Wednesday.
   He is taking the car to the garage on Friday.
2. Mrs Parker is meeting her friend Liz on Saturday.
3. Ben is going to the cinema on Thursday evening.
   On Friday he is playing basketball.
4. Sarah is visiting Karen on Wednesday afternoon.
   She is going shopping on Saturday.
5. Steve is playing tennis on Tuesday and Saturday.
6. Julie is having a ballet class on Monday and an art class on Thursday.
   On Sunday she is walking Mrs Pearson's dog.

Nicht vergessen:
Bei Verlaufsformen musst du folgende Sonderformen in der Schreibweise beachten:
- *stummes -e entfällt:*   take → he is taking
- *Konsonantenverdopplung nach*
  kurzem, betonten Vokal: sit → they are sitting
- *-ie wird zu -y-:*   lie → she is lying

Übung 2

Julie: Mum, Jackie has just called. She's going swimming in the afternoon. Can you drive me to the pool?

Mrs Parker: I'm sorry, but I can't. I'm meeting Liz at 3 p.m.

Julie: What about Dad? He surely isn't joining you and Liz, is he?

Mrs Parker: Of course not. But he is busy, too. He's putting up new shelves in his study.

Julie: That's too bad. But Ben could take me on his motorbike, couldn't he?

Mrs Parker: You needn't ask him, Julie. He's just told me that he and Emma are watching videos in the afternoon.
                    Why aren't you going by bike?

Julie: It's got a puncture, Mum.

Übung 3

Folgende Lösungen sind wiederum nur Vorschläge.
Achte auf die Übereinstimmung zwischen dem Subjekt und der Form von to be.

1. I'm meeting a good friend this afternoon.
2. I'm going to the cinema tonight.
3. My best friend and I are playing tennis at the weekend.
4. I'm visiting my grandparents next week.

8. Gegenwartsformen mit zukünftiger Bedeutung im Vergleich

Übung 1

In dieser Übung geht es um persönlich getroffene Verabredungen bzw. Abmachungen. Deshalb ist hier das Present Progressive *(mit zukünftiger Bedeutung) zu verwenden.*

Sam: Hi, Sarah. Would you like to go to the cinema with me tonight?

Sarah: I'd love to, but I can't. I'm playing tennis with Steve at 7 p.m.

Sam: That's a pity. How about tomorrow?

Sarah: I'm sorry, but Julie and I are visiting our grandparents tomorrow evening.

Sam: What about Thursday evening then?

Sarah: I think that's not possible either. On Thursday I'm helping my parents in the garden. You know, there's so much to do in spring time. But are you free on Friday? Vicky and I are going to the cinema Friday night. You can join us if you like.

Sam: Of course I do …

Übung 2

Diese Übung behandelt Kinoprogramme und Busfahrpläne, also Ereignisse, die „offiziell" festgelegt sind. Die Verbformen stehen deshalb im Simple Present *(mit zukünftiger Bedeutung).*

Nicht vergessen:

Fragen und Verneinungen im Simple Present *müssen mit* do *bzw.* does *umschrieben werden.*

Sarah: Well, which film would *you* like to watch, Vicky?

Vicky: I'd like to watch *American Beauty*.

Sam: When does it start?

Vicky: It starts at 8 o'clock in the *City House* and at 10 o'clock in the *Odeon*.

Sam: And what time does the film finish?

Vicky: Well, it lasts 90 minutes, so it finishes at about 9.30 in the *City House* and at 11.30 in the *Odeon*.

Nach Zischlauten (hier: -sh) musst du in der 3. Pers. Sing. -es anhängen!

Sarah: The last bus leaves at 11.15, which means that we can't watch it in the *Odeon*. And we really have to hurry if we want to make it in time for the 8 o'clock performance. It's already 7.25.

Sam: When does the next bus leave?

Sarah: It leaves at 7.30 and it arrives at the cinema at 7.50. Well, hurry up, folks …

Übung 3

1. "Where are you going (to)?"
2. "How long are you staying?"
3. "Are you going by coach or by train?"

Die Sätze 1–3 behandeln persönlich (von der Klasse bzw. Klassleitung) gemachte Pläne

→ Present Progressive

4. "When does your train leave?"
5. "When does it arrive in Bath?"

In den Sätzen 4 und 5 geht es um Abfahrts- und Ankunftszeiten von Zügen.

→ Simple Present

Vorsicht: „er" (= der Zug) musst du mit it *übersetzen!*

6. "Where are you staying?"

Die Entscheidung, wo Sarahs Klasse übernachtet, ist wiederum persönlicher Art

→ Present Progressive

9. Future Progressive

Übung 1

	true	false
1. Mr Parker will be having lunch at 2.30 p.m.	○	⊗
2. Mr Parker will be discussing the new project at 11.30 a.m.	⊗	○
3. Mr Parker will be meeting the new team assistant at 9 a.m.	○	⊗
4. Mr Parker will be seeing Mr Jackson before lunch.	○	⊗
5. Mr Parker will be having a sales talk in the afternoon.	⊗	○

Übung 2

> *Beim* Future Progressive *kannst du ebenso wie beim* will-Future *in der Regel zwischen* Langform (will / will not) *und Kurzform* ('ll / won't) *wählen.*
> *Wie bei allen Verlaufsformen musst du auch beim* Future Progressive *die Sonderformen in der Schreibweise berücksichtigen (s. Lösungskapitel 7).*

Next week...

1. ... I'll be sleeping in a youth hostel.
2. ... Mum won't be preparing breakfast for me.
3. ... Vicky, Karen and I will be having breakfast together.
4. ... we'll be visiting the famous Roman baths.
5. ... I'll be sending a postcard to Laura from Bath.
6. ... Sam and Daniel will be living on cheeseburgers.
7. ... Steve won't be playing tennis.
8. ... I'll be talking to Vicky for hours.
9. ... I won't be sleeping at 10.30 p.m.
10. ... Steve and I will be missing our parents.

Übung 3

1. What will you be doing tonight / this evening?
2. Will you be watching the tennis match tomorrow?
   Die Wendung "sich etwas anschauen" (→ watch sth.) ist im Englischen nicht reflexiv!
3. Will you be using your dictionary next week?
   Eine derartige Formulierung kann (muss aber nicht!) auf höfliche Art und Weise auf die Frage vorbereiten, ob du dir das Lexikon ausleihen könntest.
4. When will you be leaving the house this afternoon?
5. Will you be returning before 11 o'clock?
6. When will you be having dinner today?

> *Beachte, dass das* Future Progressive *im Deutschen mit der Gegenwart (→ Was machst du heute Abend?) oder mit dem Futur I (→ Wirst du dir morgen das Tennisspiel anschauen?) wiedergegeben werden kann.*

10. Future Perfect

Übung 1

1. Next month Mr Parker will have worked about two thousand days in this company.
2. He will have spent about three thousand hours on trains, buses and planes.
3. He will have talked to more than a thousand different customers.
4. He will have developed more than eighty computer programmes.
   Beachte, dass bei developed der Endkonsonant (-p) nicht verdoppelt wird. Der voran-gehende Vokal (-o-) ist zwar kurz, aber nicht betont. Die Betonung liegt auf der zweiten Silbe (-ve-).
5. He will have given about 250 lectures.
6. He will have travelled (→ British English) / will have traveled (→ American English) to forty European cities.

Sicher hast du gemerkt, dass du beim Future Perfect *in der Bildung der 3. Form fit sein musst.*
Hier eine kleine Wiederholung:

regelmäßige Verben	
• *Grundform + -ed:*	work → will have worked
Sonderformen in der Schreibweise	
• *stummes -e entfällt:*	prepare → will have prepared
• *Konsonantenverdopplung nach kurzem, betonten Vokal:*	stop → will have stopped
• *-y nach Konsonant wird zu -i-:*	carry → will have carried
unregelmäßige Verben	
Hier hilft nur eins: auswendig lernen!	

Übung 2

1. Will Mr and Mrs Parker have painted the front door by 11 o'clock? –
   Yes, they will have painted it by 11 o'clock.
2. Will they have taken the curtains down by 3 o'clock? –
   No, they won't have taken them down until 4 o'clock.
3. Will Ben and Steve have vacuumed the carpets by 12 o'clock? –
   Yes, they will have vacuumed them by 12 o'clock.
4. Will they have scrubbed the floors by 12 o'clock? –
   No, they won't have scrubbed them until 1 o'clock.
   Hast du an die Konsonantenverdopplung gedacht?
5. Will Sarah and Julie have cleaned the cupboards by 12 o'clock? –
   No, they won't have cleaned them until 1 o'clock.
6. Will they have dusted the furniture by 6 o'clock ? –
   Yes, they will have dusted it by 6 o'clock.

Beachte, dass furniture *im Englischen im Singular steht (im Gegensatz zur deutschen Über-setzung: die Möbel). Das zugehörige Personalpronomen ist deshalb* it.

Übung 3

1. The Parkers will have finished spring-cleaning by 4 p.m.
2. Next month the Parkers will have lived here for 20 / twenty years.
   oder The Parkers will have lived here for 20 / twenty years next month.
   Nicht vergessen:
   Im Englischen steht die Ortsangabe (here) *vor der Zeitangabe* (for twenty years).
3. Will Mr Parker have left the house by 8 o'clock?

11. Futurformen im Überblick

Übung 1

buy	going to-Future	(bejaht) (Frage)	I'm going to buy are you going to buy?
do	Future Perfect	(bejaht) (verneint)	he will have done we won't have done
arrive	Simple Present	(Frage) (verneint)	does it arrive? it doesn't arrive *Hast du an die Umschreibung gedacht?*
lie	Future Progressive	(bejaht) (Frage)	she will be lying will they be lying? *Nicht vergessen: -ie- wird hier zu -y-!*
rain	will-Future	(Frage) (verneint)	will it rain? it won't rain
stay	Present Progressive	(bejaht) (Frage)	I'm staying is he staying?

Übung 2

1. Beim Stadtbummel: „Das ist ja ein tolles T-Shirt! <u>Das kauf' ich mir!</u>"
   Futurform im Englischen: will-Future
   Begründung: spontaner Entschluss
2. Am Bahnschalter: „<u>Wann fährt der nächste Zug nach Köln?</u>"
   Futurform im Englischen: Simple Present
   Begründung: zukünftiges Ereignis, das durch einen Fahrplan festgelegt ist
3. Du träumst abends im Bett vor dich hin: „<u>Morgen um diese Zeit sitze ich im Zug.</u>"
   Futurform im Englischen: Future Progressive
   Begründung: Handlung, die zu einem bestimmten Zeitpunkt in der Zukunft abläuft
4. Du schaukelst in der Schule ganz wild auf deinem Stuhl.
   Dein Lehrer meint: „<u>Du wirst gleich runterfallen!</u>"
   Futurform im Englischen: going to-Future
   Begründung: absehbares Ereignis (für das es Anzeichen gibt)
5. Du bringst dein kaputtes Fahrrad zum Reparieren und fragst:
   „<u>Wann werden Sie das Rad repariert haben?</u>"
   Futurform im Englischen: Future Perfect
   Begründung: Ereignis, das (zu einem bestimmten Zeitpunkt) in der Zukunft bereits abgeschlossen sein wird
6. Eine Freundin möchte wissen, was du morgen machst.
   Du sagst: „<u>Meine Cousine kommt morgen.</u>"
   Futurform im Englischen: Present Progressive
   Begründung: Verabredung (in der nahen Zukunft)

12. Abschlusstest Futurformen

Übung 1

1. At 8.45 a.m. Steve and Sarah will have left Reading. They will be sitting in the train to Bath.
2. At 10.15 they will have arrived in Bath.
3. At 10.30 the allocation of the rooms will be taking place.
4. At 12 o'clock everybody will be having lunch.
5. At 1.30 p.m. they will be playing volleyball.
6. By 2.45 the class will have gone to the city centre.
7. At 3.30 they will be visiting the Roman baths.
8. At 4 o'clock they will be having a coffee break.
9. At 5 o'clock everybody will be looking at the beautiful art objects (…)
10. By 6.30 the class will have returned to the youth hostel.

Übung 2

Signalwörter sind unterstrichen!

Steve:	What are we going to do / are we doing tomorrow?
	feste Pläne in der nahen Zukunft → going to-Future *oder* Pres. Progressive*
Mr Jackson:	Well, tomorrow we are going on a sight-seeing tour first.
	Bei to go *verwendet man für Pläne das* Present Progressive!
Emily:	When does it start?
Mr Jackson:	The tour starts at 9 o'clock. Our bus leaves from in front of the youth hostel at half past eight and arrives at the town hall at eight-fifty.
	Die Stadtbesichtigung ist durch ein Programm festgelegt → Simple Present
Jenny:	What do we have to take with us?
Mrs Leech:	I think you'll need an umbrella. I've just listened to the weather forecast. Tomorrow it will be cloudy with some showers of rain.
	Wettervorhersage → will-Future
Jenny:	Oh no! I have forgotten my umbrella!
Sarah:	No problem. I'll lend you one. (…) → *spontanes Angebot*
Sam:	When does the tour finish?
Mr Jackson:	It finishes at 11.30 a.m.
Donna:	What are we going to do afterwards?
Mrs Leech:	If you want to, you can spend the lunch-break together in groups (…)
Daniel:	Great! Shall we have lunch at McDonald's?
Sam:	Good idea, Daniel! Are you going to eat seven cheeseburgers again?
	Absicht / Vorsatz → going to-future
Daniel:	If I have enough time, I will be able to eat eight or more.
	Bedingungssatz Typ I → *im Hauptsatz:* will-Future
Mr Jackson:	But don't forget to be back at the town hall at 1 p.m.
Sam:	We promise we'll be back on time. → will-Future *nach bestimmten Verben*
	By this time Daniel will surely have finished his eighth cheeseburger. Sarah, what are you doing / will you be doing / are you going to do at lunch time? → *Pläne für einen bestimmten Zeitpunkt in der Zukunft*
Sarah:	Well, Vicky and I have decided to spend the lunch-break at the river. At 12 o'clock we will be sitting on a bench in the sunshine.
Sam:	But there won't be any sunshine tomorrow … → *Wetterbericht*
Sarah:	That's a pity. But I think Vicky and I will have a nice break all the same. Without loads of cheeseburgers!

> * *Statt des* going to-Future *kannst du das* Present Progressive *nur dann verwenden, wenn der Satz eine Zeitangabe enthält, die verdeutlicht, dass das Ereignis in der Zukunft stattfindet.*

B If-Sätze
1. Grundlagen

Übung 1

1. Mr Parker / win / in the lottery   he / buy / a car / for Ben
   Bedingung   Folge
2. Sarah / go / to Sam's party   he / invite / her
   Folge   Bedingung
3. Mrs Parker / be / happy   Julie / help / her / with the housework
   Folge   Bedingung
4. Steve / work / harder   he / get / a good mark
   Bedingung   Folge
5. Julie and Jackie / not go / to the zoo   it / rain / tomorrow
   Folge   Bedingung
6. The Parkers / go on holiday / to Spain   they / have / enough money
   Folge   Bedingung

Übung 2

1. If Mr Parker hurries, he'll catch the train.
2. If I were you, I would work harder.
3. We can go outside if it stops raining.
4. Can you answer the phone if it rings?
5. If Daniel hadn't eaten eight cheeseburgers, he wouldn't have been sick afterwards.
6. Sarah would buy this skirt if it wasn't pink.
7. If you ever go to New York, you must visit the *Museum of Modern Art*.
8. Ben would be really unhappy if he didn't pass his driving-test.

> *Nicht vergessen:*
> *Ein Komma wird nur gesetzt, wenn der Nebensatz (if-clause) vor dem Hauptsatz steht.*

Übung 3

1. Sarah will take a hot shower when she returns from Bath.
   „Wenn" hat in diesem Satz die Bedeutung von „sobald". Würde man hier if einsetzen, hieße das, dass es nicht sicher ist, ob Sarah überhaupt aus Bath zurückkommt!
2. Laura will get the postcard next Wednesday if Sarah posts it on Friday.
   Hier handelt es sich um eine Bedingung: Laura wird die Karte am Mittwoch bekommen unter der Voraussetzung, dass Sarah sie am Freitag einwirft.
3. If Steve were as old as Ben, he could take driving-lessons, too.
   Ben ist und bleibt älter als Steve; der Satz handelt also von einer unmöglichen Bedingung.
4. Ben: "I need more pocket money, Dad …"
   Mr Parker: "You'll get five pounds if you mow the lawn."
   Ben wird die fünf Pfund nur bekommen, falls er den Rasen mäht (→ Bedingung).
   Ben: "O.K., I'll do it when I've finished my homework."
   Ben gibt hier einen Zeitpunkt an: sobald er mit den Hausaufgaben fertig ist, wird er den Rasen mähen.

> *Tipp:*
> *Falls du dir bei einer solchen Einsetzübung nicht sicher bist, machst du am besten immer die Gegenprobe und versuchst das Wörtchen „wenn" durch „falls" bzw. „sobald" zu ersetzen.*

2. Typ I mit will-Future

Übung 1

1. + e) If Steve doesn't hurry, he'll miss the bus.
2. + f) If you read through the text carefully, you'll be able to answer the questions easily.
3. + g) Tom will join us at the cinema if you don't mind.
4. + b) My mother will be angry with me if I don't help her with the housework.
5. + a) If you help me with the maths homework, I'll help you with the French translation.
6. + d) I will return this book to Sue if I see her today.
7. + c) If you bring some sandwiches, I'll bring some cans of lemonade.

Übung 2

Sam: Hi, Sarah. What are you doing at the weekend?
Sarah: If the weather is nice, Vicky and I will go shopping on Saturday.
Sam: And what will you do if the weather isn't nice?
Sarah: We will probably not stay at home even if it isn't sunny.
Beachte, dass probably *nach dem Hilfsverb* (will) *steht.*
But if it rains, Vicky and I will meet at my place and we'll prepare our geography paper together.
Sam: Do you need some help?
Sarah: If you are keen on that stuff, we won't send you away.
Sam: What are you doing on Saturday evening? There's a good film at the *Odeon*.
Sarah: Well, my parents are spending a day in London on Saturday. And Julie mustn't be left alone. But if they return in time, I will be able to join you.
Sam: And if they don't come back in time?
Sarah: Hm ... I've got an idea! If my parents don't return in time, we will watch some videos. Is that okay with you?
Sam: Great! See you tomorrow ...

Übung 3

Folgende Lösungen sind natürlich wieder nur Vorschläge!
Achte darauf, dass der if-*Satz im* Simple Present *und der Hauptsatz im* will-Future *steht.*
1. If the weather is nice tomorrow, I will go shopping.
2. If it doesn't rain this afternoon, I'll give a garden party.
Hast du an die Umschreibung mit does *gedacht?*
3. If my friend (Tom / Steffi / ...) visits me on Saturday, we'll go to the cinema.
Achtung: my friend = he / she → *das -s beim Verb nicht vergessen!*
4. If my parents give me more pocket money next month, I'll buy some comics / a hamster.

3. Typ I mit Imperativ oder modalem Hilfsverb

Übung 1

1. + f) If the water is too cold, we can't swim in the lake.
2. + h) Julie must put on some weight if she weighs less than 20 kilos.
3. + b) Steve can win the tennis trophy if he is in good form tomorrow.
4. + g) If we don't hurry, we won't see the beginning of the film.
5. + d) If you help me with the washing-up today, you needn't help me tomorrow.
6. + e) You must do your homework on Sunday if you don't do it on Friday or Saturday.
7. + a) If a stranger wants you to open the door, you mustn't let him in.
8. + c) Sarah can go to the cinema with Sam if Mr and Mrs Parker return in time.

Übung 2

1. If you go to* Paris, you can see the *Eiffel Tower*.
2. If you visit Vienna, you must go to* the *Hofburg*.
3. If you go to London, you must have a look at *St Paul's Cathedral*.
4. If you visit Berlin, you can walk along the *Ku'damm*.
5. If you go to Florence, you must visit the *Uffizien*.

* go to *kann im Deutschen sowohl „fahren nach" bedeuten als auch „gehen zu" (im Sinne von „besichtigen")*

Übung 3

1. If Julie gets a good mark in the maths test, she may go to the zoo.
2. If Sarah doesn't come back on time today, she mustn't go out tomorrow.
   Nicht vergessen: „nicht dürfen" heißt auf Englisch must not
3. If Steve isn't back at 8 o'clock, he can't / cannot watch the film.
4. If Ben wants more pocket money, he must help his father in the garden.
5. If the Parkers take on a housekeeper, Mrs Parker needn't do all the housework alone anymore.

Vergleiche die Wortstellung:

Wenn Ben mehr Taschengeld will, muss er seinem Vater im Garten helfen. → *Im Deutschen steht das modale Hilfsverb vor dem Subjekt; das Vollverb rückt an das Satzende.*	If Ben wants more pocket money, he must help his father in the garden. → *Im Englischen dagegen gilt die Reihenfolge Subjekt + Hilfsverb + Vollverb.*

Übung 4

1. Vergiss nicht deinen (Regen-)Schirm, wenn / falls es regnet.
   oder Vergiss deinen Schirm nicht, …
2. Räum dein Zimmer auf, wenn du deine Sachen / dein Zeugs nicht findest.
3. Hilf mir bei der Hausarbeit, wenn du nichts Besseres zu tun hast.

Übung 1

Dear Sarah,
Have you already decided when to come?
If you come in August, the weather will surely be nice.
Beachte die Stellung von surely.
If you're / you are interested in the sights of Munich, we can go on a sight-seeingtour.
But we needn't do one if you think that's boring.
If you like going for walks, we must go to the *Englischer Garten*.
If you want to buy clothes in Munich, I will show you some fantastic shops.
I'm sure that we'll have a great time together.
Write soon.   Love, Laura
Übungsvariante für Fortgeschrittene:
Decke im Übungsteil die rechte Spalte ab und versuche den gesamten Brief ins Englische zu übersetzen.

Übung 2

1. If I see her tomorrow, I will ask her whether she's got any plans for the weekend.
2. If she doesn't have / hasn't got any plans, I will suggest that we go on a cycling tour.
3. If she hasn't got / doesn't have a bike, she can borrow my sister's bike.
   In den Sätzen 2) und 3) kannst du im if-*Satz entweder* doesn't have *oder* hasn't got *verwenden.*
4. If she doesn't like cycling, I will ask her to go to the cinema with me.
5. If she wants to go to the cinema, she may choose a film she would like to see.
6. If she chooses a film I've already seen, I won't tell her.
7. If she really goes to the cinema with me, I will be extremely happy.

Übung 3

Auch diese Lösungen stellen wieder nur Vorschläge dar!
1. I'll be very happy if I get a new bike for my birthday / for Christmas.
2. If I get a good mark in my next English test, my parents will give me some extra pocket money.
3. If my sister / brother uses my computer without asking me, she / he mustn't go into my room again.
4. I'll get very angry if I find out that my friend has lied to me.
5. If it rains tomorrow, I can't play tennis.
6. I'll be thankful if my grandma gets better soon.

5. Typ II mit unwahrscheinlicher Bedingung

Übung 1

Im Hauptsatz kannst du hier, wenn dies Sinn ergibt, zwischen den Hilfsverben would, could *und* might *variieren. Beachte aber den Bedeutungsunterschied (→ würde / könnte / würde vielleicht) und überlege, was am besten passt.*

1. If Sarah cleaned her room more often, it wouldn't look such a mess.
   Hier erscheint would *am sinnvollsten.*
2. Ben would get more pocket money if he helped his father more often in the garden.
   Auch hier passt would *am besten, denkbar wären aber auch* could *(→ er könnte mehr bekommen; es liegt also in seiner Macht) oder* might *(→ er würde vielleicht mehr bekommen, sicher ist es jedoch nicht).*
3. If Steve practised even harder, he could / would / might become the best tennis player in his school.
4. Julie would have more time for painting pictures if she didn't take so many ballet classes.
   Would *ist hier wohl die beste Lösung, denkbar (mit Bedeutungsunterschied!) sind aber auch* could *und* might.
   Hast du an die Umschreibung mit did *gedacht?*

Übung 2

1. If Ben found a snake in his bed, he would kill it.
2. If Sarah found a snake in her bed, she would call the police.
3. If Steve found a snake in his bed, he would catch it.
4. If Julie found a snake in her bed, she would scream.
5. If Ben met an alien, he would say "hello".
6. If Sarah met an alien, she would ask its name.
7. If Steve met an alien, he wouldn't do anything.
8. If Julie met an alien, she would be afraid.

Schon gemerkt? – Zur Bildung von Verbformen im Simple Past *musst du fit in den unregelmäßigen Verben sein. Wie wär's mit einer gelegentlichen Wiederholung?*
Zur Erinnerung:

> *Bei regelmäßigen Verben werden die 2. und die 3. Form des Verbs wie folgt gebildet:*
> - *Grundform + -ed*
> - *Die „Sonderformen in der Schreibweise", die bei regelmäßigen Verben für die 2. und die 3. Form gleichermaßen zutreffen, findest du im Lösungskapitel 10.*

Übung 3

1. If I found a snake in my bed, I would run away and scream.
   Wenn ich eine Schlange in meinen Bett fände / finden würde*, würde ich weglaufen und schreien.
2. If I met an alien, I would talk to him.
   Wenn ich einen Außerirdischen träfe / treffen würde*, würde ich mich mit ihm unterhalten.

> ** Im Deutschen kannst du neben dem korrekten Konjunktiv (→ fände / träfe) auch die umgangssprachlichen Formen (→ finden würde / treffen würde) verwenden.*
> *Vorsicht ist bei einer Übersetzung vom Deutschen ins Englische geboten:*
> *Im Englischen darf im* if-Satz kein would *stehen!!!*

Bedingungssätze dieser Art verwendet man, wie in den Übungen 1, 2 und 4, z. B. für Tagträume und Wunschdenken.

Übung 1

1. If I had dark hair, I would look much better.
2. If I didn't have such short legs, I could wear mini-skirts.
   Durch could *wird hier stärker die Möglichkeit (→ könnte) betont;* would *ist aber auch möglich.*
3. I would be much happier if my hair wasn't / weren't* so curly.
4. If I was / were* taller, I could wear these fashionable trousers.
   Auch bei diesem Satz sind could *oder* would *verwendbar.*
5. I wouldn't be so self-conscious if I didn't have so many spots.

> ** In den Bedingungssätzen vom Typ II kann statt* was *(der für I, he, she und it üblichen Form von* to be*) auch* were *(vgl. dt. „wäre") verwendet werden.*
> *In der Wendung "If I were you …" steht jedoch <u>immer</u>* were.

Übung 2

1. If I knew Lucy's number, I would phone her.
2. If she wasn't / weren't so beautiful, I would dare to tell her (that) I love her.
3. If she was / were my girl-friend, I would be the happiest person in the world.
4. If I had lots of money, I would buy her anything she wants.

Übung 3

1. You: "If I were you, I would go / 'd go to the hairdresser's."
2. You: "If I were you, I would tell her the truth."
3. You: "If I were you, I would do a lot of sport."
4. You: "If I were you, I wouldn't buy them."

Übung 4

Wie üblich bei derartigen Übungen, sollen die folgenden Lösungen nur Vorschläge darstellen und dir als Orientierung dienen.

1. If I were eighteen, I wouldn't have to be at home at 9 p.m.
   Wenn ich 18 wäre, müsste ich nicht um 9 Uhr abends zu Hause sein.
2. If I were a pop star, I would be rich and famous / would have fans all over the world.
   Wenn ich ein Popstar wäre, wäre ich reich und berühmt / hätte ich auf der ganzen Welt Fans.
3. If I had lots of money, I would give parties every weekend.
   Wenn ich viel Geld hätte, würde ich jedes Wochenende Partys geben.

Beachte, dass die in diesem Satztyp häufig vorkommenden Verben „hätte" und „wäre" im Englischen unterschiedliche Entsprechungen haben, je nachdem, ob sie im if-Satz oder im Hauptsatz stehen. Vergleiche:

if-Satz	**Hauptsatz**
Wenn ich ein Popstar <u>wäre</u>,	*<u>wäre</u> ich reich und berühmt.*
→ If I <u>were</u> a pop star,	→ I <u>would be</u> rich and famous.
Wenn ich viel Geld <u>hätte</u>, …	*… <u>hätte</u> ich auf der ganzen Welt Fans.*
→ If I <u>had</u> lots of money, …	→ …I <u>would have</u> fans all over the world.

Um Fehler zu vermeiden, solltest du – insbesondere bei deutsch-englischen Übersetzungen – genau überprüfen, ob das Verb im Haupt- oder im Nebensatz (if-Satz) steht.

7. Typ I und Typ II im Vergleich

Übung 1

Typ I	Typ II
a) Steve and Eric can play tennis if the sun comes out later. c) If the sun shines, we won't stay indoors. f) Tidy up your room if you don't know what else to do.	b) If I were you, I wouldn't tell her secrets any more. d) What would you do if you met the Queen in the street? e) If Ben had enough time today, he could help his father in the garden.

Übung 2

1. If my grandma gives me some money, I can buy a new skateboard.
   can buy = *modales Hilfsverb im Hauptsatz* → *Typ I; hast du bei* give *an das* -s *gedacht?*
2. Sarah would / could / might phone Laura more often if it was cheaper.
   was = *Simple Past im if-Satz* → *Typ II*
3. If you help me with the washing-up, I will clean your shoes.
   help = *Simple Present im if-Satz* → *Typ I*
4. If I were you, I would tell my parents the truth.
   would tell = *Conditional I im Hauptsatz* → *Typ II*
   Nicht vergessen: In dieser Wendung kannst du nur were *verwenden.*
5. Would you mind if I opened the window?
   would … mind = *Conditional I im Hauptsatz* → *Typ II*
6. Go to your room if you keep on shouting like this.
   keep on = *Simple Present im if-Satz* → *Typ I*
   Da kein Subjekt angegeben ist, muss hier ein Imperativ gebildet werden.

Übung 3

1. a) If Eric were / was here now, we could play tennis.
   Tatsache ist, dass Steve allein ist → *unmögliche Bedingung (Typ II)*
   Statt could *kannst du auch* would *oder* might *einsetzen.*
   b) If he comes later, we will play / can play tennis.
   Es ist möglich, dass Eric später noch kommt → *Typ I*
2. a) "I would love to buy this dress if it was / were red."
   Das Kleid ist aber blau → *unmögliche Bedingung (Typ II)*
   b) "If I find a red one in another shop, I'll buy it."
   Die Möglichkeit, ein rotes zu finden, besteht noch → *Typ I*
3. a) We will go inside if it gets colder later.
   Es ist durchaus möglich, dass es später kälter wird → *Typ I*
   b) If it weren't / wasn't sunny, we wouldn't spend the day in the garden.
   Tatsache ist aber, dass es im Moment sonnig ist → *unmögliche Bedingung (Typ II)*
4. a) If Julie didn't take her doll to school, they wouldn't call her "little baby".
   Noch nimmt sie ihre Puppe mit in die Schule → *unmögliche (weil den Tatsachen widersprechende) Bedingung (Typ II)*
   b) If she leaves it at home next week, they won't laugh at her.
   Es ist aber möglich, dass sie sie nächste Woche zu Hause läßt (weil sie von den Hänseleien genug hat) → *Typ I*

8. Typ III

Übung 1

1. If Ben had had enough time, he'd have helped = would have helped his father in the garden.
2. Sarah wouldn't have gone to the cinema if she'd known = had known that it was such a bad film.
3. If he'd felt = had felt better, Steve would have won the tennis match.
4. We'd have gone = would have gone to the theatre if we'd had = had had enough money.

Alles klar?

> *Bei den Bedingungssätzen vom Typ III steht die Kurzform 'd*
> * *für* had *im* if*-Satz und*
> * *für* would *im Hauptsatz*

Übung 2

Mrs Parker: Hi, Steve. How was the match?
Steve: It was awful, Mum. I lost.
Mrs Parker: Never mind, Steve. But what happened?
Steve: It was just too hot. If it hadn't been so hot, I'd have won / would have won the match.
Mrs Parker: Why is that?
Steve: My hands were wet with sweat. If I hadn't sweated so much, I'd have hit more balls.
Mrs Parker: Did you have enough mineral water with you?
Steve: No, just one bottle. If I'd taken / had taken more water with me, I wouldn't have got tired so quickly.
And to make things worse I even forgot my sunglasses.
I'm sure I would have played much better if I hadn't forgotten my sunglasses.
Mrs Parker: Don't blame it on the sunglasses, Steve. You just had a bad day.
Steve: You're probably right, Mum. If I had been in form, I wouldn't have lost the match.

Vergleiche:

Hauptsatz	if-Satz
I'm sure I <u>would have played</u> much better → *Ich bin (mir) sicher, dass ich viel besser gespielt hätte,*	if I <u>hadn't forgotten</u> my sunglasses. → *wenn ich meine Sonnenbrille <u>nicht</u> vergessen hätte.*

→ *Während hier im Deutschen beide Verbformen mit „hätte" gebildet werden, steht im Englischen dafür* would have ... *im Hauptsatz und* had(n't) ... *im if-Satz.*
Daran solltest du insbesondere bei Übersetzungen vom Deutschen ins Englische denken!
Beachte auch, dass die Verbformen in Bedingungssätzen vom Typ III – je nach Verb – einmal mit „hätte ..." (→ I would have played / I hadn't forgotten*) und einmal mit „wäre ..." (*I wouldn't have got / I had been*) zu übersetzen sind.*

Übung 3

1. If I had gone to bed earlier, I wouldn't have overslept.
2. I wouldn't have been hungry all morning if I had had time for breakfast.
3. If I had studied enough for the maths test, I could have answered all the questions.
oder I could have answered all the questions if I had studied enough for the maths test.

9. Unmögliche Bedingungen im Vergleich (Typ II und Typ III)

Übung 1

1. If Sam had enough money, he'd buy a bunch of flowers for Sarah.
   Im if-Satz steht Simple Past → *Typ II (Bezug auf die Gegenwart)*
2. If Sam had had enough money last week, he would have bought a bottle of perfume for Sarah.
   Im if-Satz steht Past Perfect → *Typ III (Bezug auf die Vergangenheit)*
3. Ben would be sad if Emma wasn't / weren't here now.
   Im Hauptsatz steht Conditional I → *Typ II*
4. Ben would have been sad if he hadn't passed his driving-test.
   Im Hauptsatz steht Conditional II → *Typ III*
5. Julie would have painted some pictures if it had rained yesterday.
   Im if-Satz steht Past Perfect → *Typ III*
6. Julie wouldn't sit in the garden if it was raining now.
   Im if-Satz steht Simple Past → *Typ II*

Übung 2

1. If Julie found her pencil, she could draw now.
2. Steve would have played tennis yesterday if his right leg hadn't hurt.
3. If Ben didn't have such a lot of homework to do, he would / could see Emma more often these days.
   oder Ben would / could see Emma more often these days if he didn't have (…)
4. Sarah could / would have baked a cake last Sunday if she hadn't forgotten to buy some eggs.
   oder If Sarah hadn't forgotten to buy some eggs, she could / would have baked (…)

Übung 3

> *Achte beim Übersetzen darauf, dass du die „Feinabstimmungen" der Bedingungssätze (→ would / could / might) ins Englische übernimmst!*

If I hadn't been at home yesterday, he couldn't have visited me.
If we hadn't met, we wouldn't have argued.
He might not have gone if I had listened to him.
Bis zu dieser Stelle beziehen sich die Sätze auf die Vergangenheit (→ Signalwort: yesterday). Da das Gewesene nicht mehr geändert, also die Bedingung jeweils nicht mehr erfüllt werden kann, müssen hier Bedingungssätze vom Typ III stehen.
I'm extremely unhappy now.
What would you do if you were me?
I would be so happy if he were / was here now.
Die letzten beiden Sätze des Briefes beziehen sich auf die Gegenwart (→ Signalwort: now). Es handelt sich in beiden Fällen um Bedingungen, die unmöglich sind, weil sie den gegebenen Tatsachen widersprechen (Sarah kann nicht Laura sein und Jonas ist nicht hier!), deshalb musst du hier den Typ II verwenden.
Hast du daran gedacht, dass im Englischen kein Komma gesetzt wird, wenn der Hauptsatz vor dem Nebensatz (if-Satz) steht?

Übung 1

1. If Julie found a purse in the street, she'd take it to the police. → Typ II
2. Mr Parker will miss the train if he doesn't hurry. → Typ I
3. Steve might have won the match if he had been in form. → Typ III
4. If Ben has got enough money, he'll give a big party next week. → Typ I
5. If Sarah hadn't forgotten her textbook at school, she would have been able to do her homework. → Typ III

Übung 2

1. Wenn Sarah gestern zu Hause gewesen wäre, hätte Sam sie ins Kino eingeladen.
   zeitl. Bezug: Vergangenheit   Bedingung: nicht mehr erfüllbar   Typ III
   Übersetzung:
   If Sarah had been at home yesterday, Sam would have invited her to the cinema.

2. *Der Wetterbericht hat für morgen schönes Wetter und Temperaturen bis zu 27°C vorhergesagt.*
   Wenn es morgen regnen würde, könnten Sarah und Sam kein Picknick machen.
   zeitl. Bezug: Zukunft   Bedingung: unwahrscheinlich   Typ II
   Übersetzung:
   If it rained tomorrow, Sarah and Sam couldn't have a picnic.

3. Sarah wird ihre neuen Shorts anziehen, falls es morgen richtig heiß wird.
   zeitl. Bezug: Zukunft   Bedingung: wahrscheinlich   Typ I
   Übersetzung:
   Sarah will wear her new shorts if it gets really hot tomorrow.

4. Wenn Sam gerne schwimmt, kann er ein Bad im See nehmen.
   zeitl. Bezug: Gegenwart   Bedingung: erfüllt   Typ I
   Übersetzung:
   If Sam likes swimming, he can have a swim in the lake.
   Nicht vergessen:
   – _der_ See heißt "the lake"
   – _die_ See (= das Meer) heißt "the sea"

5. *Bevor Sam und Sarah am nächsten Tag losziehen, sagt Mrs Parker zu Sarah:*
   „Ich an deiner Stelle (= Wenn ich du wäre) würde (ich) ein Insektenschutzmittel mitnehmen."
   zeitl. Bezug: Gegenwart   Bedingung: unmöglich   Typ II
   Übersetzung:
   "If I were you, I would take an insect repellent with me."
   Hast du daran gedacht, dass vor einem nachfolgenden Vokal (hier i-) der unbestimmte Artikel „an" lauten muss?

11. Abschlusstest if-Sätze

Übung 1

1. Ben wouldn't go to school by motorbike if it rained tomorrow.

→ es ist unwahrscheinlich, dass es regnet

2. If Jenny comes to Ben's party, she'll bring a chocolate cake.

→ mit Jennys Kommen ist zu rechnen

3. Sarah wouldn't have got a bad mark if she had worked harder.

→ Sarah hat zu wenig für die Schule getan

4. If Vicky had known that Sarah was at home, she would have visited her.

→ Vicky wusste nicht, dass Sarah zu Hause ist

5. Mr Parker could drive Julie to the pool if he was back at 4 p.m.

→ er wird um 16 Uhr wohl nicht zurück sein

Übung 2

Sarah: Hi, Laura. How are you?

Laura: Hi, Sarah. Not too good. Are you in a hurry?

Sarah: Of course I'm not. I wouldn't phone you if I didn't have time. Why are you asking?
Sarah hat Zeit, also widerspricht die Bedingung den gegebenen Tatsachen → Typ II

Laura: Well, it's quite a long story … Jonas and I had another argument.

Sarah: Oh dear! What happened?

Laura: I was playing games on Jonas' computer when it suddenly crashed. I really felt sorry. If it hadn't been me who was playing, it wouldn't have been my fault.

Sarah: I don't think that's such a big problem. What did Jonas do then?

Laura: He called me a fool. Then I went mad and threw some CDs at him. You know, I wouldn't have thrown CDs at him if he hadn't called me a fool.

Sarah: Did they hit him?

Laura: No, the CDs missed him (…). I think I'd have felt sorry if I had hurt him.
Hier handelt es sich um drei rein theoretische Annahmen in Bezug auf die Vergangenheit (if it hadn't been … / if he hadn't called me … / if I had hurt …) → Typ III

Sarah: What did you do then?

Laura: I left at once. And Jonas didn't stop me going.

Sarah: Have you heard anything from him since?

Laura: No, not yet. And I'm sure that he won't phone me. If he phoned and said he was sorry that he'd called me a fool, everything would be all right again. But I think it's over.
Diese Bedingungen (phone / say) beziehen sich auf die Zukunft. Da sie aber unwahrscheinlich sind (… I'm sure that he won't phone me) wird Typ II verwendet.
What would you do if you were me?

Sarah: Well, I think it's not just his fault. If I were you, I would call him and ask him (…)
Sarah kann nicht Laura sein → unmögliche Bedingung in der Gegenwart → Typ II

Laura: Maybe you're right, Sarah. If he doesn't call me within the next few hours, I will call him. → *wahrscheinliche Bedingung → Typ I*
Just a second, Sarah. The door bell is ringing. If it is Jonas, I'll tell him that I'm really sorry and that I still love him …

Übung 3

Ich habe eine 4 in der Matheschulaufgabe. Iii! Wenn ich mehr getan / härter gearbeitet hätte, hätte ich nicht so eine / keine solche schlechte Note bekommen. Und vielleicht hätte ich besser abgeschnitten, wenn Mr Summer den Stoff richtig / anständig erklärt hätte. Sam sagte / hat gesagt: "Ich an deiner Stelle würde mir keine Sorgen machen. Du hast genügend gute Noten." Vielleicht hat er Recht. Wenn ich nicht nochmal eine 4 bekomme, wird in meinem Zeugnis eine 2 stehen / werde ich im Zeugnis eine 2 haben.

12. Sonderformen

Übung 1

1. + e) If you mix red and blue, you get purple. → logische Folge
2. + f) If Julie has finished her homework, she may visit Jackie.
   → Bedingung ist bereits erfüllt worden
3. + b) Laura would be sad if she hadn't made it up with Jonas.
   → Bedingung liegt in der Vergangenheit, die Folge in der Gegenwart
4. + c) If you have to learn your vocabulary, you needn't help me with the washing-up.
   → Verpflichtung in der Gegenwart
5. + d) Sam would have bought lots of presents for Sarah's birthday if he was rich.
   → Bedingung liegt in der Gegenwart, die Folge in der Vergangenheit
6. + a) Don't disturb Dad if he's working. → Bedingung ist im Verlauf

Übung 2

1. Don't interrupt Mum if she is still talking on the phone.
   Bedingung ist im Verlauf / Tätigkeitsverb → Present Progressive *im if-Satz*
   Beachte die Stellung von still.
2. If there's no battery in your personal stereo, it doesn't work.
   logische Folge → Simple Present *im Hauptsatz*
3. Mr Parker wouldn't be angry with Sarah now if she hadn't been so lazy.
   Signalwort: now (→ *Folge liegt in der Gegenwart*) → Conditional I *im Hauptsatz*
4. Steve may watch TV if he has already cleaned his room.
   Die Bedingung ist bereits erfüllt worden → Present Perfect *im if-Satz*
   Beachte: already *muss hier zwischen dem Hilfsverb* (has) *und dem Vollverb* (cleaned)
   stehen
5. If Vicky's mother can speak two foreign languages, she'll get the job.
   „können" = bestehende Fähigkeit → *modales Hilfsverb im if-Satz*
6. If the Parkers had lots of money, they would have flown to Australia last year.
   Signalwort: last year (→ *Folge liegt in der Vergangenheit*) → Conditional II *im Haupt-*
   satz

Übung 3

Falls du die Stellung von if-*Satz und Hauptsatz vertauscht hast, ist das selbstverständlich*
auch richtig!
1. If you eat too much fast-food, you get fat.
   Hier wird eine logische Folge zum Ausdruck gebracht. Im Hauptsatz steht daher das
   Simple Present.
   Vorsicht Falle: das deutsche „wird" drückt hier kein Futur aus!
   Beachte die Schreibweise von fast-food *im Englischen!*
2. Julie wouldn't be ill now if she had worn warmer clothes yesterday.
   Nicht vergessen: (Kleidung) tragen heißt wear
3. If you've translated these sentences correctly, you may call yourself a pro.
   Und? Bist du nun ein Profi?
   Die Schwierigkeiten bei der Übersetzung dieses Satzes dürften weniger bei den Verbfor-
   men liegen als bei der Verwendung des unbestimmten Artikels (a pro) *und des Adverbs*
   (correctly, *da sich „richtig" auf ein Verb, nämlich „übersetzen", bezieht*).

> *Noch ein kleiner Tipp zum Schluss:*
> *Falls du bei der Bearbeitung der Übungen auf weitere grammatikalische Probleme*
> *gestoßen bist, die du gerne wiederholen würdest (z. B. Adverbien), bietet dir der Mentor*
> *Verlag eine ganze Reihe von geeigneten Lernhilfen!*

Mentor Übungsbücher **NEU**

Das **Last-Minute-Programm**
vor der
Klassenarbeit

Deutsch

5./6. Klasse

Diktate leicht gemacht, 5. Klasse
ISBN 3-580-63810-6

Diktate leicht gemacht, 6. Klasse
ISBN 3-580-63811-4

Rechtschreibung
ISBN 3-580-63814-9

7./8. Klasse

Aufsatz: Inhaltsangabe
ISBN 3-580-63801-7

Diktate leicht gemacht, 7. Klasse
ISBN 3-580-63812-2

Diktate leicht gemacht, 8. Klasse
ISBN 3-580-63813-0

**Rechtschreibung:
Groß oder klein?
Getrennt oder zusammen?**
ISBN 3-580-63804-1

**Rechtschreibung:
Konsonanten und Vokale**
ISBN 3-580-63808-4

9./10. Klasse

Aufsatz: Erörterung
ISBN 3-580-63806-8

Protokoll und Referat
ISBN 3-580-63807-6

**Rechtschreibung:
Groß oder klein?
Getrennt oder zusammen?**
ISBN 3-580-63803-3

**Rechtschreibung:
Konsonanten und Vokale**
ISBN 3-580-63802-5

Rechtschreibung: Zeichensetzung
ISBN 3-580-63805-X

Englisch

7./8. Klasse

Adjektiv, Adverb, Substantiv, Pronomen
ISBN 3-580-63854-8

Die Zeiten – Bildung und Verwendung
ISBN 3-580-63851-3

If-Sätze und Futurformen
ISBN 3-580-63855-6

9./10. Klasse

Die Zeiten – Bildung und Verwendung
ISBN 3-580-63852-1

If-Sätze und Futurformen
ISBN 3-580-63856-4

Mathe

8. Klasse

Bruchterme und Bruchgleichungen
ISBN 3-580-63901-3

9./10. Klasse

Quadratische Gleichungen und Ungleichungen
ISBN 3-580-63903-X

Wurzelterme und Wurzelgleichungen
ISBN 3-580-63902-1

**Je 80 Seiten, mit Lösungsteil
zum Heraustrennen**

Mentor
Eine Klasse besser.